THE WAY OF AN INTERCESSOR

The Way
of an
Intercessor

AUDREY MERWOOD

KINGSWAY PUBLICATIONS
EASTBOURNE

ISBN 0 86065 339 0

Biblical quotations are from the
Revised Standard Version, copyrighted 1946, 1952,
© 1971, 1973 by the Division of Christian Education of the
National Council of the Churches of
Christ in the USA

AV = Authorized Version
Crown copyright

GNB = Good News Bible
© American Bible Society 1976

TLB = The Living Bible
© Tyndale House Publishers 1971

Front cover design by Vic Mitchell

TO RAY
with love

Printed in Great Britain for
KINGSWAY PUBLICATIONS LTD
Lottbridge Drove, Eastbourne, E. Sussex BN23 6NT by
Cox & Wyman Ltd, Reading
Typeset by Central Southern Typesetters,
Eastbourne, E. Sussex.

Contents

Foreword

It is a joy and privilege to commend this book to all who would seek to walk the way of an intercessor. In the history of Israel when 'every man did that which was right in his own eyes' God raised up the intercessor and the prophet, and so it is today that he is raising up an army of intercessors throughout the nations. With so many situations that need our prayers – where do we begin? Surely by getting as close to him as we can, so that as we know the mind of Christ, we can pray in the power of the Holy Spirit.

From her own experience Audrey shares in an honest and practical way her call to intercede, and some of the many lessons she has learned along the road, and I know she would be the first to admit she is still learning.

Are only special people called to the place of prayer? Audrey is a busy wife and mother, working alongside her husband in the vicarage, and one who knows the blessing of a life fully yielded to her Lord. She heard the call, she responded; that is all we are asked to do. She shares principles that have changed her life and the lives of others, as she has been obedient to wait on God and pray his prayers for them.

It is my prayer that all who read this book may know a deeper desire to wait on God to know his heart, and pray his prayers for the church, our own nation and the world.

CHRIS LEAGE
National Co-ordinator (England)
Lydia Fellowship

Acknowledgements

My name appears on the cover as the author of this book, but although I did the actual writing many other people have contributed in different ways to its production, and I should like to express my deepest thanks to them all.

First, to my husband, Ray, for his loving support and encouragement from the moment the idea for the book was born and for giving me the freedom to write it.

To Jeanne Harper and Chris Leage, for much personal encouragement, and to the Lydia National Team (UK) in 1982, who, with Jeanne and Chris, waited on the Lord for direction concerning this book. Also to Chris for reading the manuscript and making helpful observations and suggestions.

To Barbara and Richard Steele-Perkins for reading the manuscript, chapter by chapter, as it came fresh from the typewriter, and for all their helpful comments and suggestions.

To John Wood, who read the completed manuscript and with zeal and a great sense of humour pointed out errors of punctuation and grammar – and other disasters.

To Shelagh McAlpine, for helping me with information about the beginning of the Lydia Fellowship and for her comments on chapter 2.

Special thanks to two people who lightened the load of domestic chores, my lovely 'extra' daughter, Susie Williams, who did the housework and cheerfully went the extra mile, and my friend, Beryl Holland, who often moved mountains – of ironing and washing up.

My thanks also to all my family and friends who have prayed for me and encouraged me, and to Margaret Crawford, Vera Jeffery, Barbara Steele-Perkins, Noreen Govier, Dorothy Bradshaw, Joan Thomas and other Lydias, who have taught me more than they know.

And above all to my heavenly Father, for the privilege of being an intercessor.

An Enlarged Place

Enlarge the place of your tent, and let the curtains of your habitations be stretched out; hold not back, lengthen your cords and strengthen your stakes.   (Is 54:2).

'Dear God, please bless Mummy and Daddy and all my brothers and sisters . . . .' So began the prayers which I said as a child, every night. Simple and to the point they were, and I never doubted for one minute that God heard them, that he was interested in what I had to say and that he would comply with my request. I knew he was there – I'd always known – and before I hopped into bed I would thank him for all the good things and ask him to keep us safe through the night, and to send his holy angels to guard us.

I think my mother must have taught me to pray almost before I could talk, because searching back into the earliest memories of childhood one of my strongest and most constant recollections is of 'saying my prayers'. As I grew older I began to learn that not only was God someone who would look after me and listen to me, but he also had something to say to *me*. Prayer was a two-way business. Just thinking about it I experience again the thrill I felt when I realized that God had plans for me, and if I would listen he would tell me about them. I could ask questions and get answers! I began to ask different things, too. I still asked him to keep me safe, to bless the people I loved, but I also began to ask him, 'Lord, what do you want me to do?' And I listened. I wanted to know what he thought about things. I was learning to wait on God.

As children we may come to our earthly father and say, 'Daddy, may I . . .? Daddy, will you . . .?' and be pleased if we get what we ask for, but children quickly learn what pleases or displeases their parents, and where there is an example of love they soon want to give as well as receive. Moreover, they want to be involved in whatever Daddy is doing – they want to help.

As we grow, our earthly father not only allows us to help, but trusts us to do things for him. To begin with he may take us by the hand when he goes to the corner shop to buy the daily paper, but there comes a day when he is able to send us out *on his behalf,* to bring the paper home for him. He has shown us the way and he knows we can, and will do what he asks of us.

I believe that our prayer relationship with God is rather like that. Whether we have known him in childhood, or have come to know him later in life, we all go through a spiritual childhood. In those early days our prayers are very likely to be simple requests, not only for things, but for guidance, for comfort and for strength. But as we grow and mature, as we begin to experience God in the fullness of the Trinity, we find that, although we may still bring our own requests to him with that childlike simplicity, he now begins to lead us on to a wider and deeper experience of prayer. If we desire to please him and be available to him, then we have truly begun to live the life of prayer.

God is our Father, and he made us for himself; he loves us, cares for us, and wants us to choose to be part of his eternal purpose.

He is Jesus, at once our Lord and our Brother. We inherit with him the privilege and authority of *sons* (Rom 8:15-17). He has gone before us, and he walks with us. Everything we are ever going to experience along the way he has already experienced. We can know him, and keep company with him, while at the same time he continually prays on our behalf before the throne of grace (Heb 7:25; Rom 8:34; 1 Jn 2:1).

He is the Holy Spirit, who comes with enabling power; with insight, knowledge and understanding. It is he who teaches us to pray: 'He will teach you all things' (Jn 14:26), if only we will trust him.

Prayer is a mystery from the beginning. *Why* should God, who made all things without our aid, actually choose to work through our prayer, inviting us to be a part of his eternal purpose? We may not be able to answer this question, but we know from experience that it is true. He does invite us, and he longs for our ready and unconditional response. If we give him our heart's unconditional surrender, he brings us to an experience of oneness with him, and involvement in his purposes, which is more exciting and more beautiful than anything we could possibly have dreamed up for ourselves.

Several years ago, when I was seeking the Lord's direction at a time of change in my life, the words at the head of this chapter became strongly impressed upon my mind. God often speaks to us directly and personally through a passage of Scripture, and I sensed that he was doing so then, though what it could mean I just did not know. What was all this about enlarging the place of my tent and stretching out the curtains of my habitation? Did it mean our home was to be more open? Our family extended?

During the next few years we were indeed to receive some unexpected and needy people into our home from time to time, but I came to see that God was talking to me about making myself open and available in an even wider sense. The people I was going to embrace in my 'enlarged place' and beneath my 'stretched out curtains' were going to be far more numerous than those we could receive into our home. I would have to learn not to hold back, no matter how new and surprising the things God asked of me; my cords would indeed need to be lengthened (that is, my vision widened), and my stakes certainly needed strengthening to make me secure and unshakable in the adventure that was to come.

What I was hearing, in fact, was God's call to be an intercessor, though it was some time before I understood. In the following weeks I found myself wanting to spend more time in his presence, to *hear* him. I wanted to know what he was saying. And gradually, as I yielded my will to his, I began to gain understanding. In my little prayer notebook I wrote down on several occasions, 'God wants me to wait on him for other people.' Now as I understood it, the phrase 'to wait on him' meant to seek him and to ask for his direction and guidance in any matter, and to wait for this before taking any action. I could do this for myself – but for other people? How could I seek guidance from the Lord on their behalf? And what if I received this guidance? Should I go to them like some prophet and say, 'Thus says the Lord . . .'?

Slowly I began to realize that he wanted me to *pray* for people, not as I had prayed before from the limited resources of my own understanding, but to wait on him for the understanding of his purposes and his direction, and so to pray according to his will. The Holy Spirit was teaching me the basic principles of intercession: first, to allow him to tell me who to pray for, and then to let him tell me how to pray. It sounds so simple put like that – obvious even. Yet it came as a revelation to me, and it led me into an experience of prayer which has been, and still is much, much more than anything I had expected.

I soon began to understand that I was to intercede not only for people I knew but even for people I had never met and never would meet; people in high places and in desperate circumstances alike; in our own land and in distant lands. Gradually the Lord put into my heart a deep desire to pray for the people of this nation and of other nations of the world, a longing to have his understanding, to feel the pain and the compassion of his heart for this sick and sorry world, to be an instrument in his hand, a channel of his love.

But me? How can I pray like that? Yet if you say so, Lord, I will.

The way of an intercessor can be a way of loneliness, but God does not ask us to go it alone all the time. In fact it is part of his plan that we should come together to pray. Before very long I met other women who had heard God's call to be intercessors, and I began to learn with them that this challenging and exciting activity was to be a life-changing thing. There is so much evil and sorrow in the world, and often in the lives of those close to us. But God is King of all the earth – it is his world. The battle and the victory are his. He calls all of us in some way to be part of the spiritual battle against evil, and some of us he calls to take part in this particular way – to be intercessors.

But that is only a beginning. When we say yes to God's call, whatever he may be asking of us, he begins to change us, to make us ready, to make us holy. Often the deep work of love and inner healing which the Holy Spirit works in his children as a result of that yes comes as an almost overwhelming surprise. We come expecting to do battle on behalf of the King of kings – and find that some of the most amazing changes and victories take place in us! Cardinal Suenens has spoken of the 'Holy Spirit's surprises', and that's just what they are: the healing of mind and spirit as well as body; the release from bondage (often previously unrecognized); the restored and renewed relationships and the blossoming of personalities.

Then, as we learn to trust God, the Holy Spirit is able to lead us into new ways of prayer beyond that which many of us have known before. Our whole concept of prayer expands to the extent that we trust God and do what he tells us. He is able to give us discernment and understanding in situations both close at hand and in faraway places, beyond our knowledge and natural understanding, to lay upon our hearts his own desire and compassion for those we are to pray for, and to express our prayer in new and unexpected ways.

PART ONE

'Not Against Flesh and Blood . . .'

For we are not contending against flesh and blood, but against the principalities, against the powers, against the world rulers of this present darkness, against the spiritual hosts of wickedness in the heavenly places.

Eph 6:12

I

Possess the Land

When I first realized that God wanted to lead me into new ways of prayer I did not immediately understand all that he was saying. I had learnt that prayer was a two-way thing – God had things to say to me as well as I to him – but the idea that he wanted me to *do* something in prayer was quite unknown to me. I had understood prayer as *coming in* to God's presence, to speak to him and to listen to him; to praise and worship him; to receive from him guidance, strength, comfort, whatever my soul needed, and to ask for others what I perceived they needed. It was still very much a matter of asking and receiving. I had now to learn that it could also mean *going out* on his behalf, doing something 'in his name', at his direction, and therefore with authority.

In the beginning God put into my heart a new awareness of the plight of other people. I began to feel compassion, in the truest sense of the word – that is to say, grief and sorrow mingled with a longing to do something to relieve the suffering and confusion which I saw. Of course I had always been concerned, but this was something more. It was a pain in my heart for the nations. Sometimes we talk about 'the church' as though it has an identity all of its own, apart from ourselves, forgetting that *we* are the church. In the same way we often speak of 'the nation' as though it too has its own separate identity. Of course it hasn't. The nation is people. Living, loving, working, striving people – and often suffering people. Why, in this complex, wonderful world which God has created, is there so much confusion and misery? There arose in me a desire, almost a desperation, to have God's understanding of these things, to feel as he feels and to share in his compassion and love for this groaning and travailing world. This was the very basis of the call to pray.

The call to be an intercessor was, for me, followed very quickly by a call to be part of a fellowship of intercessors, and I began to discover that many people were feeling as I did. Having found one fellowship of intercessors, I heard of another, and another, a whole army of people called and committed to pray for our nation and the nations of the world. I suppose till then I had considered this kind of specially committed and dedicated prayer to be something that went on mostly in monasteries and convents, where they had time for that sort of thing. But now I saw that the call to prayer can come to anyone. I began to understand that God wanted me to join with other people to do something on his behalf by means of our prayer, and that to intercede meant to make ourselves available to him for the prayer he himself would give us. It meant praying as he directed and, with his authority, coming against those forces of evil which are at the root of the world's misery and suffering. For the first time in my experience the term 'spiritual warfare' began to have a meaning.

If an army was sent out to fight without knowing that there was a war on, it would be a hesitant and uncertain venture indeed. The ordinary soldier will not always know all that is going on, but he needs to know that he *is* at war, that there is a battle to be fought, and an enemy at large. Furthermore, he needs to know who that enemy is and to be able to recognize him. There is no time or place in warfare for hesitancy or uncertainty. More still, he must know and understand how to use the weapons of war that are placed at his disposal, and above all he must recognize and trust the one from whom he is to receive orders.

What has this to do with us? Are we at war?

Yes we are. Every person who commits himself to Christ immediately puts himself into a battle situation. Having joined the ranks of the Lord of light we are at war with the powers of darkness – we are involved in the fight between good and evil.

All through the ages, from St Paul onwards, the Christian church has been depicted as an army, and one very much on active service.

Timothy is exhorted to 'wage the good warfare' (1 Tim 1:18) and to be a 'good soldier of Christ' (2 Tim 2:3). In the letter to Philemon, Archippus is referred to as 'our fellow soldier'. Writing to the Corinthians Paul says, 'We are not carrying on a worldly war,' and speaks of the 'weapons of our warfare' as having 'divine power to destroy strongholds', presumably enemy strongholds (2 Cor 10:3-4).

'Put on the whole armour of God,' says Paul in the passage which introduces this section. 'For we are not fighting against human beings, but against the wicked spiritual forces.' And again, 'Put on God's armour now!' (Eph 6:11-13 GNB).

A soldier does not dress up in battle gear unless he is going to fight!

The hymn writers take up the theme: 'Soldiers of the Cross, arise . . . mighty are your enemies . . . hard the battle ye must fight.'

'Onward, Christian soldiers, marching as to war . . . forward into battle . . . .'

'Soldiers of Christ, arise,' says Wesley, 'and put your

armour on . . . Wrestle, and fight, and pray . . . Tread all the powers of darkness down and win the well fought day.'

No army on standby this, but an army marching; soldiers in full armour, banners unfurled.

Clearly there is a war on.

In a war everyone is expected to resist the enemy in every way he can, even perhaps to take up arms at some point. However, not everyone is called into the armed forces. As a teenager in the Second World War I belonged to what was called the Girls' Training Corps. I learnt to recognize enemy aircraft and tanks in case we should be invaded, and during that time I was also given some rudimentary lessons in how to handle a rifle – though whether I would ever have shot anyone is very doubtful indeed! Mercifully, the enemy stopped at Calais and I was never put to the test. My main contribution to the war effort was the work I did in a factory, plus some weekends spent serving tea and buns to soldiers and airmen in a church canteen; and a few unknown servicemen were warmed, I hope, by the balaclava helmets and scarves which I knitted on my bus journeys to work and home again.

Everyone has to be ready in time of war to turn a hand to whatever is required of them from time to time. Yet at the same time each person has his or her own specific job to do. It is just the same for the church, the army of God. In the spiritual fight against evil, every single one of us is on active service. This means that each one of us must be alert and ready to do anything which God may require of us at any time, but it also means that, within his perfect plan for the conduct of that fight, he is calling and equipping each of us to play our own particular part.

In his letters Paul refers to some of the many ministries which are to be exercised by different people within the church. It is clear that we are not all called, for example, to exercise a specialized ministry of healing, though the Holy Spirit may direct any one of us to use this precious gift at some time in our lives. We are not all prophets, though many of us will be used to give a word of prophecy at some time. Similarly with the ministry of intercession, which is a calling as clear, unique and positive as that to be a teacher, pastor, evangelist or anything else. Everyone is required to pray all the time, and sometimes to intercede (see Eph 6:18; 1 Tim 2:1), but for some of us it is a specific and specialized ministry.

To be an intercessor is costly in terms of time, commitment, availability and obedience. It also requires humility, for it is mostly a quiet, even secret work. There are no honours or recognitions. If God is calling you, be prepared for your work to be hidden and unacknowledged for the most part (here on earth at any rate).

In military terms the intercessors may be seen as something like the S.A.S., who go into a situation secretly, often under cover of darkness, to prepare the way. Nobody knows they are there, or where they've been, and nobody knows who they are (they don't tell!), though the enemy certainly knows they've been! Without the work of these special units it would often be difficult, if not impossible, for the rest of the army to do its work effectively.

Or they may sometimes be seen as the artillery, whose job it is to put up a steady and concentrated barrage against a specific enemy stronghold, until the defences are weakened and it is possible for others to go in and 'take the city'.

So, in spiritual warfare, the intercessors are the ones who go before; they are the pinpointers of objectives; the bombarders of enemy positions; the demolishers of strongholds. They are support and cover for others who go into many different and dangerous situations. They are also watchmen, ever on the alert. I shall be elaborating on this in later chapters, and we shall see what it means in practice.

The use of military language in connection with prayer may seem rather daunting, but it is valid. However, though we are undoubtedly an army, our weapons and methods of warfare are as different from those of a worldly army as light is from darkness. This also will become clear as we go along.

What, then, is the nature of the war in which we are engaged, and who is the enemy?

The army of which we are a part is a victorious army, there can be no doubt about that. Jesus Christ, the Son of God, our Saviour, by his death upon the cross and his glorious resurrection from the dead has opened the gates of hell and let the captives free. He has, once and for all, won the victory over sin and death. 'Christ, being raised from the dead, will never die again; death no longer has dominion over him' (Rom 6:9).

This is an irreversible fact.

Everything we do, therefore, is done from a position of victory. In the closing stages of the Second World War, when the Allied Armies had landed in France and were painfully pushing the enemy back and overcoming him, there were some terrible battles. We knew the end was in sight. The enemy was in disarray and the outcome was inevitable, but he was still fighting. The war was won – and yet it was not over. There was still much to be done. The enemy was still in control of many places. He had to be rooted out of every nook and cranny in which he had a foothold. It would have been no good, at that stage, for the Commander in Chief to have said, 'It's all right, lads, it's all over. You can go home now.' That would have been to hand back to the enemy all that had been won at such a cost.

No! There were enemy units to be rounded up and disarmed; imprisoned people to be set free; the stinking hellholes of Belsen, Auschwitz and others to be found, opened up and cleansed; and somehow peace and order had to be brought to a tortured continent as it strove to rebuild sanity and normality into its daily life.

Even such a mighty and terrible war as that cannot parallel, or even truly illustrate, the one in which we are engaged. The Second World War, along with all the other wars and battles that have ever been and will ever be fought on this planet, is but another episode in the context of the mighty conflict between the forces of good and evil, but it does to some degree serve to illustrate the position in which we find ourselves.

Yes! We do belong to a victorious army, the supremely victorious army of all time, and these times are the closing stages of the war. Jesus has finally and irrevocably overcome Satan and all his hosts. He has put the foe to rout. 'Death's mightiest powers have done their worst, and Jesus has his foes dispersed.'

The enemy is in disarray and has no power over us – *except that which we allow him to have.* Jesus has given us the victory, and at the sound of his name, Satan and all his hosts flee. We are free – and that also means free to do what we will with that victory. We can choose to sit cosily by our own firesides and pretend to ourselves that everything is now all right. Or we can face up to the fact that there is still something to be done. It would have been no good for the Allied Armies in Europe in 1945 to have ignored the pockets of resistance, still less to pretend that Belsen wasn't there. They had to go right into that terrible place – enemy territory as it still was – and come to grips with the evil and suffering they found there, and to set free those poor souls who did not even know that the war was over. The war was won, but somebody had to go in and possess the land.

Now look around you.

You may be enjoying a degree of satisfaction, with

food in your belly and clothes on your back, but else-where in the world people for whom Christ died are starving to death, in nakedness and squalor, every day.

You may know the Lord Jesus Christ as your Saviour; you may worship in your church every Sunday, but else-where many people are still in the darkness of ignorance and superstition, in bondage to fear of evil spirits.

You may go freely to your chosen place of worship; you may go freely about your work and your pleasure. Your brothers and sisters in other places are not free to worship as they choose; many, under the curse of apar-theid and other repressive regimes, may work and live and have their being only where and how they are per-mitted to do so by their oppressors.

You may have a happy, stable family life, a good mar-riage with a loving partner. Your children may be happy, well adjusted and secure in the love of their parents. But you don't have to look further than your own town, probably your own street, to see families disrupted, chil-dren suffering the loss of a parent, bewildered and div-ided in their loyalties. Even in this so-called Christian country men and women have turned away from the righteous and loving laws of God, with disastrous conse-quences. A whole generation is growing up for whom one-parent families, sexual 'freedom', homosexual re-lationships, abortion and VD are commonplace – as are violence and bloodshed, in real life and in fiction, to which that latest phenomenon the 'video nasty' is mak-ing an ever increasing contribution.

There are still women selling their bodies and men using and exploiting them; pornography and drugs are peddled and more lives for whom Christ died are brought to corruption and ruin.

More and more people, seeking some satisfaction, not knowing the Lord Jesus Christ and his saving grace, are being drawn by one means or another into occult practices, seemingly harmless to begin with perhaps, but binding them ever more tightly and surely, so that they cannot escape until someone comes to set them free.

Even as I write these words the guns are blazing in that torn and unhappy land of Lebanon, and by the time you read them who knows where the next conflict will have broken out, as nation rises against nation in suspicion, distrust and fear?

I do not wish to underrate the good, the beautiful and the true in ordinary men and women of good will, nor the joyfully triumphant lives of those who acknowledge Jesus as Lord, but wherever these evil conditions exist and these things happen, the enemy has his footholds – strongholds even – and his Belsens.

Clearly, there is still a war on.

It is the work of the church – Christ's own army of occupation – to go in and possess the land, and in that work, as we have begun to see, the intercessors have a special and very specific part to play.

'And God saw everything that he had made, and behold, it was very good' (Gen 1:31).

'For in him [Christ] all things were created, in heaven and on earth, visible and invisible, whether thrones or dominions or principalities or authorities – all things were created through him and for him. He is before all things, and in him all things hold together' (Col 1:16-17).

If everything that God made was 'very good', and all things were created through Christ and for Christ, and if everything and everyone must acknowledge his lordship (Phil 2:10-11), who is behind all the misery and suffering in the world? Who is the enemy?

Paul makes it clear (Eph 6:12) that this is no ordinary enemy, for 'we are not fighting against flesh and blood' (that is, ordinary human beings). It is the devil – that fallen angel, referred to in Isaiah as 'Day Star, son of Dawn' (Is 14:12) and in Ezekiel as having been 'the sig-

net of perfection, full of wisdom and perfect in beauty',
until, because of his pride and vanity, he was cast from
the mountain of God as a 'profane thing' (Ezek 28: 12-19).

Paul goes on to list other malevolent agencies, 'principalities and powers . . . world rulers of this present
darkness . . . spiritual hosts of wickedness in the heavenly
places'. Who are they?

The dictionary defines a 'principality' as the rank, or
state, of a prince, and also the territory over which he
rules that gives him his title. It is an interesting fact that
one of the Hebrew words translated as 'prince', used
with the particular sense of one 'exercising dominion,
whether as supreme or subordinate to an overlord', is
also used for *angels,* particularly the guardian angels of
countries (Dan 10:13, 21 for example).

The New Bible Dictionary (Inter-Varsity Press) refers
to an angel as being of an order higher than that of man,
'a creature, certainly, but also holy and uncorrupted spirit
in original essence, yet endowed with free will, and therefore not necessarily impervious to temptation and sin'.

Therefore, as with man, it is possible for an angel to
'fall', and there are enough references in the Bible to tell
us that this has in fact happened. In Job we read of God
charging his angels with error (Job 4:18), or finding 'fault
even with his angels' (GNB). Jesus spoke of the 'eternal
fire prepared for the devil and his angels' (Mt 25:41). In
2 Peter 2:4 we read, 'God did not spare the angels when
they sinned . . .' and in Revelation 12:9 that, 'Satan, the
deceiver of the whole world – he was thrown down to the
earth, and his angels were thrown down with him.'

It seems to me that the principalities referred to by
Paul are those areas (both geographical and otherwise)
wherein these angels, in rebellion against God, have
found their habitation, where they 'exercise dominion'
under the overlordship of Satan himself. They have become 'world rulers of this present darkness' and com-

mand 'spiritual hosts [armies] of wickedness in the
heavenly places'. These are not the forces of some independent superior being, they are God's own creatures in
rebellion against him, and just as their creation was 'in
Christ', so also was their defeat (Col 2:15).

I am greatly indebted to Michael Green for a better
understanding of these matters, which he deals with
comprehensively in a chapter entitled 'Principalities and
Powers' in his book *I Believe in Satan's Downfall* (Hodder
& Stoughton).

Jesus Christ came into the world with the express purpose of destroying the works of the devil (1 Jn 3:8) and it
is absolutely essential that we, his church, his body, his
army, should recognize and understand the nature of the
warfare in which we are still engaged; that we should
know the real power and influence behind the perse-
cutors and the workers of ill upon earth.

Having said that, it is vital that we keep this whole
area in proper perspective. We must recognize Satan and
all his minions for who they are, and with God-given
discernment see clearly both the extent and the limitations of their power. We must not attach to them the
blame which should rightly be laid at the door of mankind's own unwillingness to make a judgement between
right and wrong, nor attribute to them authority and
power which belong to God alone. We must earnestly
desire and seek from God this discernment, to know
what is of him, what is human and what is truly satanic.
As Michael Harper has said:

> It is a hard road to travel, and calls for constant vigilance,
> and a closeness to our Lord which is sacrificial, disciplined,
> at times dangerous, and unpopular with some.

It is this road that the intercessors are called to travel.

It is worthwhile reminding ourselves, before we move
on, that anyone who deliberately and knowingly con-

tinues in sin is giving the devil and his agents a foothold – he or she is in a very real sense 'harbouring the enemy'. It is important to realize this and be on our guard.

Identifying the enemy is the first step. It is immediately obvious that no ordinary warfare will suffice against this enemy. 'The weapons of our warfare are not worldly, but have *divine power* to destroy strongholds' (2 Cor 10:4).

Paul speaks of the spiritual hosts (armies) of wickedness as being 'in the heavenly places' (Eph 6:12) and the New Bible Commentary points to the parallel with Ephesians 2:2, the church's conflict being seen in both passages to be located in 'the upper air regions', the precise region which is 'also the sphere of Christ's rule (cf 1:20), the consequent fountainhead of God's blessings upon his people (cf 1:3) and the place where the wonders of what God is doing through the church are being made known (cf 3:10)'.

This puts the conflict firmly in the realm of the spiritual. To understand the church's part in this conflict, and the work of intercessors in particular, we must grasp the concept of another dimension. At some point, if we are truly to live a life of prayer, and certainly before we can fully embark upon the work of intercession, we have to come to terms with mystery, to accept the fact that not everything can be weighed, analysed and assessed by our finite minds. We do not need to know the why or the how. It is enough for us to trust the Holy Spirit and allow him to extend the boundaries of our experience in prayer.

'Lord, teach us to pray,' said the first disciples. We must go on saying that, and allow him to lead us into realms perhaps as yet unknown to us. As we do so we shall grow and mature in our understanding of our position and authority as sons and daughters of God, charged with the awesome responsibility of going in to possess the land – reclaiming enemy territory on behalf of the King of kings.

2

Do Whatever He Tells You

There is nothing new about the call to prayer. The work of prayer has been carried on faithfully, obediently, patiently, by believers – both individually and corporately – right through the ages. What is significant now, I believe, is the extent to which God is raising up people of prayer, and the importance within his plan of the small groups of people, deeply committed to him and to each other, who will meet regularly to pray as he directs.

Right at the heart of our response to any call to a work of God must lie simple obedience. Simple – but sometimes oh so difficult! To be obedient means to be *ready and willing* to obey; it means yielding to another's will, in this case to God's will. I love that word 'yielding'. It implies a softness, a flexibility, so that I will bend to the will of God, even though he may ask me to do something I would not have chosen to do. And although something may, as yet, be outside my experience, I will not hold back. I will open my heart and mind to whatever he sets before me; I will allow my vision to be widened – my 'cords lengthened'.

In the early days, while I was still seeking to understand more fully what it was God wanted me to do, I was invited to a women's rally. There were two speakers, whose names will be familiar to many, Jeanne Harper and Joyce Tait. These two women spoke of love, unity and prayer in a way that I had never heard before, and it was during one of their talks that for the first time I heard mention of the Lydia Fellowship. Something was already stirring within me in response to what I was hearing, and at the end of that session I went to the back of the hall to look at the literature there for those who were interested. At random I picked up a leaflet and opened it, and the very first words that met my eyes were, 'Enlarge the place of your tent, and let the curtains of your habitations be stretched out.' It was the very verse of Scripture (Is 54:2) with which God had first shown me that I was on the brink of something new, and that there was more to prayer than I had yet known. I gazed down at the leaflet in amazement, and I knew that God was saying to me, '*I* have brought you to this place, to hear these words, for a purpose. This is to be your work from now on.'

That was my introduction to 'Lydia' and I was so eager to learn more. My first lesson was patience! A little time was to elapse and a few things in my life were to be sorted out before I would be part of a praying group.

I shall be saying more later about the forming of prayer groups, but in this chapter I want to share just a little about the Lydia Fellowship, within the general context of God's call to his people to pray.

God wanted to do a work among women. His purpose was to call them to the place of prayer to intercede for revival in church, community and country, and as part of his plan to bring this about he chose a faithful woman of prayer, Shelagh McAlpine. In March 1970, in obedience to the Lord and with the co-operation of her husband, Shelagh invited a group of women to their home to hear her friend, Joy Dawson, speak on the principles of intercession. Although Shelagh may not have realized it at the time, from that small beginning was born a fellowship of praying women which was soon to spread not only throughout this country, but far beyond its shores.

> And on the sabbath day we went outside the gate to the riverside, where we supposed there was a place of prayer; and we sat down and spoke to the women who had come together (Acts 16:13).

So it was that Paul and Silas in Philippi met Lydia, who worshipped God and prayed there. Luke tells us that God opened her heart and that she made herself and her home available to the apostles (Acts 16:14-15, 40). Surely it is significant that before long prison doors were opened in that city, where prayer was being made by the believers, including an open-hearted woman and her companions. It seems fitting that Lydia's name should have been given to a twentieth-century fellowship of intercessors.

This book is in no way a 'history' of the Lydia Fellowship, how it began and how it has grown. That story belongs to Shelagh and to those women who were privileged to be there at the beginning with her. I could not possibly write it. Nor am I attempting to set out the overall, world-wide vision of Lydia, with all its aims and purposes.

I have only a tiny part to play in the whole but, like countless others, I have 'caught' the vision. I believe God wants me to share what being an intercessor means to me and many others; to tell of the ways in which it has changed our lives; and to share some of the new things in prayer to which we have been led by the Holy Spirit.

A little while ago I heard the Lydia Fellowship described as: 'The fastest growing work of the Holy Spirit in the country today.' Whether or not that is true, there can be no doubt at all that Lydia is a mighty work of God, and the contribution it is making to the great body of prayer being offered, and to the church's corporate understanding of what intercession is about, is immeasurable.

But Lydia is not the whole story by any means. Not only are others joined together in prayer fellowships (as in Intercessors for Britain, for example), but the word 'intercession' is on the lips of Christians everywhere in these days, as groups of men and women within local churches and across denominational lines respond to the call to pray, especially to pray for the church, our nation and the nations of the world.

It has been said that when God wants to do something he first sets his people praying. The call to prayer has never, I think, been stronger, or clearer, or more urgent. Nor has the response been more ready. And what is vitally important is that we should all be obedient to whatever God gives to *us*. 'Do whatever he tells *you*' (Jn 2:5).

I believe there are certain basic principles of intercession which the Holy Spirit is teaching us all. We should all seek his guidance as to who or what to pray for, and how to pray, but as we allow him to lead us and to build upon the foundation of these principles, if we find we are being led in slightly different ways from other people, we should heed our Lord's words to Peter when he wanted to know what John should do; 'What is that to you? Follow me!' (Jn 21:22).

No one has a monopoly on the guidance of the Holy Spirit, and just as we need to keep the reality of spiritual warfare in the right perspective, so also we must have our own part in that warfare in the right perspective too. Our prayer forms part of a rich and glorious tapestry of prayer offered to God by his people throughout the ages. The difficulty for us is that at the moment we can only see the 'wrong' side of the tapestry. How awful it would be if we were to ruin the pattern because we were bothered about someone else putting in stitches different from our own! Let us faithfully put in our own stitches, as God directs, and leave the rest to him. In the fullness of time we shall see the 'right' side of the tapestry, and marvel not only at the beauty but at the effectiveness of God's design.

Although we cannot see the whole, it is evident that a very important part of God's design is the formation of many small groups of people for the purpose of intercession. I think we can see at least some of the reasons why this should be so.

To start with, we have our Lord's own words: 'Where two or three are gathered in my name, there am I in the midst of them' (Mt 18:20). I am sure this is not meant to put a limit on how many people should come together! Christ's promise to be present applies as much to large gatherings as to small. However, he can work in different ways through different kinds of gathering.

For the 'special missions' which the intercessors are called upon to undertake, it is necessary for us to be able to relate to one another in a close and intimate way which is not possible in a large gathering. We need the love and trust which can grow between people as they get to know each other really well, and we benefit from the fellowship and support which each gives to the others in the group.

From a purely practical point of view, it is necessary for us to share with one another the thoughts and ideas given to us by the Holy Spirit as we wait upon him in preparation for our prayer, and there is a limit to the size of a group in which this kind of sharing would be possible. Through this sharing we are able to check with one another what the Spirit is saying, so that we come to an agreement, a common mind. 'Again I say to you, if two of you agree on earth about anything they ask, it will be done for them by my Father in heaven' (Mt 18:19). This agreement is a fundamental necessity in the work of intercession and it brings with it a strength and confidence without which it would be folly to move out into spiritual warfare.

As a group we have a commitment, first of all to the Lord who has called us, and then to each other to make ourselves available to him together for the appointed times of prayer. This commitment should never be entered into lightly, but only after waiting upon God and knowing that this is what he requires of us. Having been entered into, it cannot be lightly set aside. However, there will inevitably be some occasions during which, according to the will of God, one of us will have to be engaged elsewhere. Because we are a group it means that the work of prayer goes on at the appointed time and in the appointed place, unhindered by temporary illness or other things which may arise from time to time.

In the Lydia Fellowship each prayer group has its own identity and seeks to be led by the Holy Spirit in its prayer, while at the same time it forms part of a larger fellowship under the leadership of a national team. Area leaders and Teams have a special responsibility for the groups in their locality. I like to think of this as many living cells gently held together within a flexible membrane – not restrictive, but supportive and uniting. In this way it is possible for the leaders and teams to exercise a pastoral care for the groups and for individuals; to help and advise in the birth of new groups; to be aware when God is requiring us, either nationally or in one or two specific areas, to engage in a corporate act of prayer and to co-ordinate this. We all benefit enormously from the conferences and area meetings which take place from time to time. These are occasions for encouragement; for invaluable teaching; for enlarging our vision; and often for personal ministry and the resolving of some of the problems which sometimes arise. They are also often occasions for corporate times of intercession.

Sooner or later, when Lydia is being discussed, somebody asks, 'Why only women?' The answer, as given to me by Shelagh McAlpine, is that the vision of Lydia was given specifically for women, and her call and anointing as the founder of the fellowship has been to work within the boundaries thus set by God.

Perhaps when we come together to pray *as women* God is able to make use, in a special way, of those insights and attributes which are essentially feminine, and doubtless he can do something equally special with those essentially masculine characteristics when men meet together. Whatever his reasons for the ways in which he is doing it, God is calling many people, both men and women – sometimes separately, sometimes together – to be his intercessors. It is noticeable, however, that a very great number of women are being called to this work. Chris Leage is the present English national leader of the Lydia Fellowship, and she travels a great deal with other members of the national team, visiting the areas and speaking at meetings. I have heard her relate how, on their many journeys, they have encountered scores of women who were hearing God's call. Many of them had never heard of Lydia, but God himself had implanted within them a deep desire to pray for our nation and others, and they were responding.

A short while ago an old lady died in Jerusalem. She was Mother Barbara, Abbess of the Russian Orthodox Convent on the Mount of Olives. When Mother Barbara was a young girl she was taken on a visit to Russia, and there, in 1911, a monk gave her the following prophecy:

An evil will shortly take Russia and wherever this evil comes rivers of blood will flow. This evil will take the whole world and wherever it goes rivers of blood will flow because of it. It is not the Russian soul, but an imposition on the Russian soul. It is not an ideology or a philosophy but a spirit from hell. In the last days Germany will be divided in two. France will be just nothing. Italy will be judged by natural disaster. Britain will lose her empire and all her colonies and will come to almost total ruin, *but will be saved by praying women*. America will feed the world, but will finally collapse. Russia and China will destroy each other. Finally, Russia will be free and from her believers will go forth and turn many from the nations to God. [Italics mine.]

This amazing prophecy has been an encouragement to many women as they have become aware of God's call to them, and the deep desire to pray for the nations.

3
Where Two or Three Are Gathered

The call to intercession begins with a deep desire to pray, and often this is accompanied by a realization that we do not know *how* to pray in certain situations. There is a cry from the heart: 'Lord, how can I pray? Show me what to do.' Usually, too, people begin to realize that they need someone to pray with. Christ has promised to be present with us whenever we meet together in his name. He will direct our prayer, and that direction starts right at the very beginning, with the formation of our intercession groups.

At the meeting where I first heard about the Lydia Fellowship, a young friend of mine was also present, and her response was much the same as mine. After the meeting she came to me and said, 'Well, what about it? Are we going to start a Lydia group?' We knew each other fairly well, and had been praying together in a prayer and Bible study group in our parish for some time. It would have been the easiest thing in the world, and quite natural, to have said, 'Yes, let's get started.' There didn't seem to be any reason why not, but I just felt a check in my spirit and surprised myself rather by saying instead, 'Debbie, I somehow feel we should wait a little while and pray about it some more. Perhaps later on we could meet and see what we think then.' She accepted that, and during the next few months the Lord kept her pretty busy with other things. Meanwhile, she prayed and I prayed.

One day, when the whole matter was very much on my heart, I was alone in the house, walking up and down, just asking the Lord what he wanted me to do about it, when the thought came to me, 'I must talk to Dorothy about this.'

Confident that this was the answer to my prayer, I telephoned Dorothy and fifteen minutes later she was at our house. Over a cup of tea I shared with her what was on my mind. Imagine my surprise and delight when she revealed that she had been on the point of raising the matter with me, as she felt this was what God wanted her to do. We arranged to meet to pray again about this call from God, and before long we were meeting regularly to pray. That was the beginning of our intercession group. In the fullness of time others, including Debbie, were added to us, but during the months when Dorothy and I prayed alone I began to understand why God had sent us to each other first. I had such a lot to learn and it was through the gentle, loving and wise ministry of Dorothy that God had chosen to minister to me, to teach me and encourage me. Indeed, we had much to give each other in those early days, which was to form the basis of a loving, trusting relationship upon which to build an intercession group.

It has to be true that any two or three Christians can come together to pray if they want to, but forming a deeply committed unit for the purpose of regular, un-remitting intercession requires rather more in the way of preparation. I sometimes think it is like making a pudding . . . .

If a cook changes one or more of the ingredients in her pudding, with a degree of success or failure according to her experience and skill she may end up with a 'good pudding', but it will not be what its inventor intended. It is well worth while taking the trouble to get the 'ingredients' in our intercession group right and waiting for God to lead us to the prayer partner or partners of *his* choice. This has nothing to do with a spiritual elitism, nor with personal fancy – some people have been very surprised at who God has led them to – but it has everything to do with the fact that God knows our personalities better than we do. *He* knows precisely what gifts each one of us will bring to the common experience of the group. If we do it his way, the mix will be right. All we have to do is to listen to God; to be sensitive to the promptings of our own heart, to the word spoken by another which may be the sign we have been waiting for; and we shall know his direction. Then all will be well, as it was with Dorothy and me, and ultimately with the rest of the group.

Many prayer groups start very small and grow gradually, and that seems to be the best way, the way God does it. But however small a group may be to begin with, it is well to ask God from the beginning who is to lead it. Here again sensitivity is needed to the direction of the Holy Spirit, and we must be clear about what we mean by 'leadership' in this context. It is not that one person will be set apart by God to 'direct operations', to turn up with a list of things to be prayed for. The essence of a group of this kind is that *together* we wait upon God and *together* we receive from him the direction on what to pray for and how, but it will quickly become clear that someone has to co-ordinate things. Furthermore, while we all care for each other, there will be one person who has a special responsibility for a pastoral oversight of the whole group. Often it will be fairly obvious who the leader is to be – perhaps the person who initiated the forming of the group in the first place – but it is worth saying here that the leader is not necessarily the 'strong' member! Leadership has more to do with gentleness and patience, with insight and understanding and, perhaps most of all, with that priceless gift of being able to encourage others to blossom into all the fullness of what God desires for them. True leadership is not concerned with the ability to sweep others along on the tide of its own ideas and enthusiasm. So do not seek leadership, but pray about it, the two or three of you who start. God has his own ways of making his choice apparent, which we often speak of as the anointing of the Holy Spirit, and if we are open to his direction we will recognize this. Once you know who is to lead the group, give her your full love, support and confidence, and pray for her, as she also will for you.

When and where you meet will depend, of course, upon the circumstances of those in the group, but it is important to find a place and time in which you can be comfortable and undisturbed. This is usually in someone's house. If other members of the household are at home during the time of meeting, you will need to explain that you do not wish to be disturbed, and why, and arrange for someone to take any telephone messages for you. If you have to answer the door or the telephone you can briefly explain that you are engaged and offer to contact your caller later – people who call upon you unexpectedly ought to understand this. If there is no one else at home and the milkman is likely to call for his money, leave him a note and arrange for a neighbour to pay him for you. Attention to a few simple details like this can make all the difference, and there is certainly nothing 'unspiritual' about efficient organization! Generally speaking, you are not to be disturbed.

'Children,' said our Victorian forebears, 'should be seen and not heard.' What a hope! It is difficult for little children to be still and quiet for any length of time, so if one or more members of a group has children of pre-school age this will be another thing to take into consideration. Evening meetings may well be the simplest answer, or perhaps there will be another friend who, though not called to the ministry of intercession herself, may see as her contribution to the work the running of a crêche for the group. Grandmothers and aunts, if they live near enough, are usually more than willing to help out, and these visits can become regular treats much looked forward to on both sides. People vary a great deal in how much they are distracted by the presence of small children – during church services and on other occasions – and I believe it is worth while trying to make arrangements for the little ones to be looked after. However, this may not always be possible and I know there are a number of groups who manage very well with the children around. The Holy Spirit is the enabler, and if you are called to intercede, and your hearts are set on being available to him, your prayer will not be hindered. If there is anyone who really finds herself too distracted, then perhaps she should ask the Lord if he would have her in another group.

Unhurried time is another very important consideration when we are making our arrangements. If you can meet for most of a day, say from about 9.30 in the morning till about 3 or 4 in the afternoon, this is excellent. For some this is not possible and it may be that a whole morning or afternoon is the answer, or perhaps an evening. I have heard of some groups which, though normally managing only a morning or an afternoon, are able to make special arrangements and have a whole day together every month or so.

Decide realistically how often you can meet and stick to your decision. If it really becomes clear after a while that it is difficult to keep to your arrangements, then you will have to pray again and revise them, but usually, if you have prayed about it in the first place and been honest with yourselves and each other about what is realistic, you will soon settle happily into a regular routine. What's more, your family and friends will know, too, that you are committed at these times and therefore not available for other things, and that can save a lot of problems.

Satan does not like prayer, and he most certainly does not like intercession, for, properly understood, intercession is a direct attack upon enemy strongholds. Therefore he will do anything and everything to undermine our work. We shall be seeking direction from God and we need to make sure we hear him and him alone. The enemy will tap and cut our lines of communication if he can. It is up to us to make sure we are prepared and equipped to hear God and to carry out his instructions.

Our preparation begins long before we come together. It begins in our own individual times of waiting upon God; in our individual commitment to him and our response to whatever he asks of us. It begins in our willingness to be broken, melted and moulded into the person he wants us to be; in our simple obedience concerning the plain, ordinary things of everyday life and our readiness to be realistic and diligent in making the kind of practical arrangements I have outlined above.

When we begin to make preparation as a group we shall be carrying on together from where we have each arrived individually, gathering up our separate threads and weaving them into a strong cord.

The first thing to think about in the way of preparation is fasting. This is something which, again, you will need to pray about individually beforehand, so that you all know what you are doing. Intercession and fasting go together. There is power in fasting. If the idea is completely new to you, do not be dismayed. Throw out any ideas you may have of a stern and harsh asceticism. Fasting is a strong discipline, but it can be learnt gradually, and there are several ways of doing it. God will show you what is right for you, in your particular circumstances, and as you become used to it and it becomes a regular part of your way of life, you will discover unsuspected benefits.

Perhaps you wonder why we should fast. The first part of the answer is, because Jesus obviously intended that we should. Speaking to his disciples he said, 'When you give alms . . . when you pray . . . when you fast' (Mt 6:2, 5, 16). *When,* not if, and we are included in those instructions. Christ's great commission to the apostles, after his resurrection, was to make disciples of all nations, teaching them to observe all that he had commanded.

I was brought up to fast. In the tradition of the church to which I belong it was the accepted thing always to come fasting to Holy Communion (except during times of sickness), to eat little during Holy Week, and to fast altogether on Good Friday and some other 'holy days'. It did me no harm! Indeed, it did great good, for it was a discipline which laid the foundations for what was to come in my life later on. But in those earlier days that's all it was – a discipline; one that I accepted and felt better for, but never fully understood. Then one day, during a special time of prayer, I became aware that the Holy Spirit was directing me to fast, only somehow what I then understood as fasting didn't seem to be adequate. I couldn't see what he was getting at, but by this time I had come to recognize these sometimes puzzling promptings of the Holy Spirit as indications that he wanted to teach me something.

Sure enough, before very long, my attention was caught by a book which one of my daughters was reading, *God's Chosen Fast.* This book, written by Arthur Wallis, was to prove one of the most interesting books I had ever read, and I was surprised to realize just how much of this important subject I had missed in my reading of Scripture. The Bible is full of example and precept – Moses, David,

Elijah, Daniel, Ezra, Esther, among others; and in the
New Testament, Anna, who worshipped 'with fasting
and prayer night and day' (Lk 2:37), and Saul and others
at Antioch worshipping and fasting, fasting and praying
(Acts 13:2-3). There is only space in this book to consider fasting specifically in connection with intercession,
but it is well worth while taking time to make a proper
and wider study of it. Arthur Wallis's book is still available (published by Kingsway Publications).

Fasting, as we are considering it now, means abstaining from food for spiritual purposes. Going without
something, especially something as basic and normally
necessary as food, seems at first to be totally negative,
but our motive here is to *give to God,* and that is positive.
By our willingness to go without food, either completely
or partially, for a period of time, we are declaring to God
(and to the enemy) that we mean business. We are letting go of the needs and desires of the flesh in order to be
completely available to God in body, mind and spirit.

It is interesting that when we use that last phrase we
nearly always seem to put 'body' first. The flesh is ever at
war with the spirit, and an undisciplined body usually
leads to a dull mind and a flabby spirit.

Mahatma Ghandi, and other political leaders, have
used fasting as a kind of passive resistance. In more recent times we have seen the awful hunger strikes of Irish
political prisoners, but this is far removed from what we
are talking about. We are not trying to twist God's arm
to get him to listen to and answer our prayer. Far from it!
When we fast *unto God* we are *giving* to him. When we
wake up on the morning of a day of fasting, we should
approach it with joy, thinking: 'This is the day that the
Lord has made; we will rejoice and be glad in it.' After
reading Matthew 6:16-18 we should come to prayer not
demanding or expecting anything for ourselves, but
knowing that the Lord our God loves to bless and to

honour our sacrifice.

In practice it is common experience among those who do undertake this discipline for definite spiritual benefits to follow. As intercessors we are totally dependent upon God for the direction of our prayer, for 'we do not know how to pray as we ought', and fasting is an effective and speedy way of making our minds receptive to the revelation of his will in a situation about which we are praying. This is often one of the first noticeable benefits (see Acts 13:2-3; Dan 9:3, 21-23). Jesus warned us of the coming of false prophets, with signs and wonders, who would 'lead astray, if possible, even the elect' (Mt 24:24). Satan is the master of confusion and deceit, and he will draw distractions across our path whenever we give him the opportunity. As we shall see a little later on, it is necessary for all our own ideas and convictions, however sincerely held, to be laid aside in the time of prayer, that we may hear what God wants to say to us. Fasting truly helps us concentrate the mind on God alone.

If we are to be effective intercessors we need to know how to exercise the authority given us by Jesus. 'Behold, I have given you authority . . . over all the power of the enemy' (Lk 10:19). 'Whatever you bind on earth shall be bound in heaven, and whatever you loose on earth shall be loosed in heaven' (Mt 16:19; 18:18). But we cannot command the enemy if we are not in command of ourselves, and this is often the reason for our lack of authority over Satan and his minions. We are conscious of our ineffectiveness and doubtful about our commission, like 'a wave of the sea that is driven and tossed by the wind' and 'unstable in all its ways' (Jas 1:6-8).

An athlete preparing for a race disciplines himself; he 'exercises self-control in all things' (1 Cor 9:25). He 'tones up' his body in order to win a perishable prize. By the discipline of fasting we tone up spiritually as part of our preparation for spiritual warfare, confirming within ourselves the intention to be fit and ready in every way for what God requires of us and demonstrating to the enemy that we really do mean business.

People who are reluctant to accept a discipline such as this often try to explain it away by redefining it to suit themselves. Fasting, they will tell you, means exercising self-denial; getting rid of anything that comes between us and God; going without something that has become very important to us; and so on. All these things are right and necessary, but the Oxford Dictionary defines fasting as going without food. A study of the biblical examples of fasting confirms this quite simple definition.

A normal fast, therefore, will consist in going without food (solid or liquid) and drinking only water. If you have never done this before it may be well to begin by missing out one meal. Omitting your evening meal, for example, would result in a fast of about eighteen hours. Next time you could try missing your lunch and your evening meal, and eventually going without food for a whole day, which, counting the two night periods, would result in a fast of about thirty-six hours' duration. After that you will find it possible to fast for longer periods, but always this must be done at the direction of the Holy Spirit and very definitely taking into account any medical requirements.

A partial fast (or 'Daniel' fast as it is sometimes called) may consist of abstaining from solid food, but taking liquids (soup, milk, tea, coffee, etc), or it may consist of abstaining from certain kinds of food only (see Dan 1:10-15; 10:3). This kind of fast is useful for people who have some kind of medical problem which would make a normal fast unhealthy or dangerous. To abstain from only certain kinds of food is also a good method for a prolonged fast when it is necessary at the same time to keep to a full working programme. It was to a fast of this kind that God led me as a result of my first reading of

Arthur Wallis's book. I undertook a 'Daniel' fast for one month, during the course of which I was completely healed of a very troublesome condition which had afflicted me, on and off, for over thirty years.

The absolute fast consists of taking no food or water. This is a very strict discipline and should never, in any circumstances, last longer than three days.

Usually a normal fast, or perhaps a partial fast – taking just soft drinks, tea or coffee – will accompany our regular times of intercession, and the duration of this will depend upon circumstances, health and so on. As in all our preparations and arrangements, the Holy Spirit himself will guide us if we ask him. It may not be possible for every member of the group to fast in the same way or for the same length of time, but what is important is our motive. We must offer our fast to God in humble, loving obedience, desiring thereby to come closer to him, to gain a deeper understanding of his word, to receive his direction for our intercession and increased authority and power as we pray. We should, at all times, avoid ostentation (see Mt 6:16-18), or any kind of legalism. During these times we may well be the subject of spiritual attack from the enemy, tempting us to feel proud or superior. Or, it may be quite the opposite, to feelings of unworthiness, doubt, and to all manner of subtle distractions. Be on guard for these attacks and deal with them swiftly and with authority.

All plans have been made; you arrive at the appointed place at the appointed time. How will you start?

Some groups may like to come in quietly and get straight down to business, but for many it is not a bad idea to have a cup of tea or coffee together (if your discipline of fasting permits this), allowing time for greetings and the exchange of recent news. This removes all those thoughts in the back of your mind such as, 'I must remember to tell Mary . . .', and there may be information to share which will be relevant later on. All this need take no longer than fifteen minutes, and then you are ready to begin.

What I offer next are some simple steps of preparation for an intercessory group, which many people have found effective. They are not intended to be legalistic, and certainly not ritualistic, and groups who use them will vary in the ways in which they apply them. But if used as a guide and a pattern they do help us to lay aside our own anxieties and ideas, focussing all our attention on God so that we may receive his direction and not be sidetracked by the craftiness of the enemy.

4

Coming In . . . and Going Out

First know your Lord and proclaim him

Let there be no doubt in anyone's mind as to who is in charge of the whole operation. Jesus is Lord! So make it known. To proclaim means to announce publicly, to declare openly. So do it. Declare it as a truth about your own life, that Jesus is Lord. Acknowledge to each other that he is Lord of this gathering, the place where you meet, of the time you have set aside. Speak it out loud, in words and in song. You will not be talking to yourselves. The demons hear and quake. The angels hear and make merry in heaven!

This proclamation may be lively and robust, or it may be very gentle and quiet, but always it must be sure and confident. There are many lovely songs which can be sung at this point, and a little study of the Psalms will provide beautiful and helpful words to read or recite. If you have someone to lead you with a guitar, or on the piano, so much the better, or perhaps someone is confident enough to lead straight into a song or a hymn. It is surprising how good at this you can become, if you only have the courage to try once or twice! Another helpful thing, in the absence of any musicians, is for the leader to choose a suitable song on a cassette and just to play this as a starter.

One or more people may call to mind a verse of Scripture, or even a short poem, which proclaims the lordship of Jesus, and they can speak this out. Or it may be that you will feel moved to speak short sentences of your own, or say out loud some of the titles of God: Wonderful, Counsellor, the Mighty God, Everlasting Father, Prince of Peace; Jehovah-Elyon (God Most High), Jehovah-Shammah (God is there), and so on. While you are doing this, feel yourself relaxing in the presence of the Lord.

Be cleansed

Any known and unrepented sin will stand between us and our Lord; it will prevent us from hearing him and our prayer will be rendered ineffective before we have even begun. Psalm 66:18 says, 'If I had ignored my sins, the Lord would not have listened to me' (GNB). So these things should be dealt with immediately. We should have been before the Lord alone in penitence for any known sin; but it is well at this point to ask the Holy Spirit to shine into the dark corners of our hearts and reveal anything which may still be lurking there. As people who are about to intercede, look out for self-effort, unbelief, and fear. It is usually best for the leader, or another member of the group, to invite the Holy Spirit to come and do this, and then to wait in silence while he does it. Here again, a few short, appropriate verses of Scripture – perhaps from a psalm – may be helpful as an introduction to this part of the preparation. 'Examine me, O God, and know my mind; test me, and discover my thoughts. Find out if there is any evil in me and guide me in the everlasting way' (Ps 139:23-24 GNB). (See also verses 1-6.) 'The Lord watches over the righteous and hears their cry' (Ps 34:15 GNB).

Although this part is done in silence, apart from the

reading of Scripture, sometimes it may be helpful to speak out a short prayer, in general terms: 'Lord, help thou my unbelief.' 'Help me to forgive, that I may be forgiven.' Occasionally, if we are conscious of anything wrong between ourselves and another member of the group, especially if we are unforgiving, it may be good to go quietly to that person and ask their forgiveness, and assure them of ours. When you are ready to proceed, look up, so that the leader will know, and now, together, joyfully receive and acknowledge the cleansing and the forgiveness of God. 'He is faithful and just, and will forgive our sins and cleanse us from all unrighteousness' (1 Jn 1:9). 'His mercy is on those who fear him' (Lk 1:50), or 'He shows mercy to those who honour him' (GNB). 'Bless the Lord, O my soul; and all that is within me, bless his holy name. Bless the Lord, O my soul, and forget not all his benefits, who forgives all your iniquity' (Ps 103:1-3).

It is important to do this, to make real to ourselves the wonderful mercy of God. Jesus has paid the price for our sin; it is in *his* righteousness that we are made acceptable and able to come before the throne of grace. Satan loves to make us feel unworthy, and therefore useless. Don't let him! Stretch out your hands (if you find this helpful), as you would when someone gives you something, and say to the Lord that you receive his love. And know that it is done.

Be filled with the Holy Spirit

Now, at once, let someone ask for the Holy Spirit to come upon you all in his fullness; to fill you; to surround you; to direct you; to pray through you (Rom 8:26).

'Come, Holy Ghost, our souls inspire . . .,' 'Take our minds and think through them; take our lips and speak through them; take our hearts and set them on fire with love for thee.' 'Lord, we receive your love, we receive your Holy Spirit, we are filled.' (See Acts 2:17; 4:31; 2 Cor 1:22; Gal 4:6; Eph 1:13.)

Take every thought captive to obey Christ

We cannot pray the prayers that God is waiting to give us if our minds are cluttered up with our own troubles, family problems, or fears. The purpose of our meeting together in this way, as intercessors, is to make ourselves available to God for his wider purposes and not, at this time, to deal with our own needs. Our own needs are important, of course, but we must be able to lay them aside for the time of intercessory prayer. This can be done quite simply. The group leader may now invite us to do this, and perhaps she will read something like 1 Peter 5:7, 'Cast all your anxieties on him, for he cares about you,' or Psalm 55:22, 'Cast your burden on the Lord, and he will sustain you.'

Most of us have something on our minds most of the time. Therefore it is good to be specific at this point. Maybe there is a sick child at home, a husband has just been made redundant; the cistern overflowed last night and brought the ceiling down; you've overspent the housekeeping money and you know your husband is short this month too – the list of woes and worries is endless! It may be enough to just silently – and specifically – name all these things to the Lord. Or, in a close-knit group like this, it may be helpful to briefly name them out loud. 'Lord, I leave Johnny in your hands today, and I know Auntie May will take good care of him.' 'I commit Harry to you.' 'I know you will help me sort out the money later on.' In this way we can, as it were, help each other to lay down our burdens. But whether you do it silently or openly, *do it*. It may help if you remind yourselves that all the while you are physically present at the meeting place you cannot *do* anything about your problem, so worry and thought are unproductive anyway.

I remember once attending a Girl Guide entertainment in which one of our teenage daughters was taking part in a sketch based on Bunyan's *Pilgrim's Progress*. She was Christian, and there was one splendid moment when she staggered on to the stage bearing over her shoulder an enormous bulging sack – her 'burden' of sins and sorrows. She made her way, apparently with great difficulty, to the centre of the stage and there she heaved the sack over her shoulder and dumped it at the foot of the cross. Then she demonstrated her great sense of release. That little scene often passes before my eyes when I come to this part of the preparation, for I often feel just like she looked that evening, and, being thus reminded, I know exactly what to do – take it all to the foot of the cross and *leave it there*.

Occasionally, however, someone will find it very difficult, or impossible, to set aside a burden, and if this is the case the person must say so and something must be done about it before you proceed, otherwise she will not be able to hear the Lord and the whole group will be affected. If the problem is very personal and private, then she can explain that this is so, and without knowing the details the leader, with the rest of the group, can pray for her. The leader can ask the Lord to assure her of his continuing love and care for her and for the person for whom she is anxious, binding Satan, declaring the lordship of Jesus in her life and in this particular situation, and asking him to set her free now from anxiety in order that she may serve him in this time of intercession. If the problem is one that can be shared, then you could pray specifically about it.

During a residential conference I was asked to lead a group for a time of intercession. At this point in the preparation I prayed for the families left at home, and several other people also spoke out simple sentences, committing people and things to God's care, but when I asked if everyone was happy to move on, one woman, who had never prayed in this way before, said, 'It's no good, I simply cannot do what you ask. How can I stop thinking about my children?' and she burst into tears. She then shared with us some very serious problems which she was having at that time with her teenage children. She didn't go into a lot of detail, but she wanted us to pray for her. I asked her to kneel down and two of us laid hands upon her. Then we prayed for each of her children by name, asking the Lord to keep them. We took the authority given to us by Jesus and bound Satan and all his minions, declaring the lordship of Jesus in her life and her family's. Then for a few minutes we continued to pray quietly in tongues, until this turned into gentle praise. The burden was completely lifted from her and we were able to continue. The whole thing had taken only a few minutes, but afterwards she told me it had been one of the most wonderful experiences of her life. 'I never knew it was possible to forget my own problems like that,' she said, 'and to be so single-minded for God.'

If we went into deep or prolonged ministry at this time we should probably never get down to intercession, and how the enemy would love that! If he can divert us from our purpose by something as obviously good and worth while as that, so much the better for him! The time for ministry is not now, but a brief 'holding' prayer in the way I have described should be all that is necessary to set the person free. On another occasion the leader, and one other member of the group, may be able to provide the necessary ministry, or to encourage the person to see her vicar or pastor, or some other wise counsellor, to get the matter dealt with. This is where the pastoral care of the leader for each member of the group is so important.

It is not only our *problems* that can get in the way. We cannot pray effectively, either, if our minds are full of our own ideas and foregone conclusions about the rights and wrongs of any given situation, about what or who we should be praying for, and what we should be asking. If the Holy Spirit has been laying any particular thing upon our hearts very strongly during the days preceding the day of intercession we may share this with the rest of the group, not with the idea that we *must* pray about it, but rather that together we may come to a common mind. We shall be meeting to pray as he directs on the appointed day, but sometimes he does prepare us beforehand, and in this case we usually find that more than one person has had the same prompting from him. The important thing is not to be anxious. The thing you are so concerned about may have been given to someone else to pray about. We can think again, here, of the tapestry of prayer. God has the overall design. You put in the stitches he gives you and leave the rest to him, confident that somebody else will be covering the other matters.

So, as well as that great sackful of worries and fears, lay down at the foot of the cross all your much cherished, preconceived ideas about anything whatsoever. I think it is almost harder to part with these than with our anxieties! Give God your mind. This is where prejudice gets dealt with – whether racial, religious, or any other kind – and political bias, and this is so important when we are praying for the nation.

God does not want us to bypass our minds, of course, but he does want us to consecrate them to him. We all have political convictions, but we are not met to pray against some unfortunate politician whose election day rosette is a different colour from our own. We are met to share God's heart and his longing and desire for his people and for all the people of the world, and to pray according to his desire for those he gives specifically to us.

Therefore, down at the foot of the cross must go all those strongly held views of ours. 'Take my intellect and use every power as thou shalt choose.' It would be good to pray that prayer every day, and especially in the days leading up to a time of intercession.

Our knowledge and prayerfully thought-out opinions will not be wasted. God will make use of what is in each mind *as he needs it.* Only let it be truly consecrated to him. In his hands it will be a sharp and effective tool. In our own hands it may well be a dull and clumsy bludgeon.

We have 'come in' to the presence of God, to surrender ourselves to him, to make ourselves available to him, and it is good to be unhurried about this preparation so that it is done completely. The amount of time we can spend upon it will depend to some extent upon whether we have a whole day or only part of a day for our prayer, but it is possible to be unhurried and recollected about this even when we have only a short time, and this is very important. The leader should make sure that you do not move from one point to another until everyone is ready.

Now it is time to consider 'going out', but we are not quite ready for that yet. There are one or two important steps to be taken before we can safely enter into spiritual warfare, and the first of these is to avail ourselves of the equipment which God has provided for us – to 'put on the whole armour of God' (Eph 6:11). No commander worthy of the name would send his troops to battle without first making sure that they were properly equipped, and God is the Supreme Commander. The equipment he has provided for us is specially designed for the job we have to do – for engaging in spiritual warfare. 'For though we live in the world we are not carrying on a worldly war, for the weapons of our warfare are not worldly but have divine power to destroy strongholds' (2 Cor 10:3-4).

Again let me emphasize that this is not meant to be,

nor should it ever become, an empty ritual. Look at it this way. My friend comes into my house bearing a gift for me. She places it upon the table between us, saying, 'This is for you.' She has now given me something, but no matter how valuable or useful the gift may be in itself, it is of no use whatsoever to me as long as it remains there upon the table. I have to take the gift, to appropriate it and make it my own. So what we are doing when we 'put on' or 'take' the whole armour of God is making a spiritual appropriation of what God has given us.

The church teaches that a sacrament is 'an outward and visible sign of an inward and spiritual grace', as for example in baptism and Holy Communion, and we are 'sacramental' beings. God has made us this way, which means that we do need, and benefit from the outward expression of that which is spiritually discerned and received. In this sense a kiss or a handshake may be said to be 'sacramental', and although what we are doing in this preparation is not a sacrament as in baptism or Holy Communion, yet it does have a sacramental nature in that it expresses, and enables us to make our own, that which God has given us.

Put on the whole armour of God

The girdle of truth

With this piece of equipment we are reminded, and we declare, that we are sons of God through Jesus Christ, and it is in *his* kingdom we live, not that of Satan.

This knowledge protects us from all the lies and false accusations of Satan. Satan is 'a liar and the father of lies' (Jn 8:44), and he is also the 'accuser of our brethren' (Rev 12:10). The sin of unbelief, which we mentioned earlier, may be due to listening to, and being taken in by Satan's lies about God. The sense of unworthiness and ineffectiveness which we so often experience comes from accepting Satan's lies about ourselves. He, Satan, will also do his utmost to lead us into error. So buckle on the girdle of truth and render him powerless in this area.

The breastplate of righteousness

It is in the righteousness of Jesus, and by the power of his blood shed for us on Calvary, that we are made holy and acceptable, to come in to the King of kings (Eph 1:4; 5:27; Col 1:22). Put on this breastplate as protection against all evil thoughts and sinful desires of the flesh, for be well assured that if Satan cannot deceive us with his lies he will seek to lure us with his subtle temptations and worldly desires, and perhaps the desire to be super-spiritual. Of ourselves we are weak, but in the right-eousness of Jesus we are inviolable (2 Cor 5:21; Rom 3:21-26).

The shoes which are the equipment of the gospel of peace

In the days when an army marched, its shoes were a vital piece of equipment. They would have to be good to give them a firm footing when the ground was rough and uneven, and to keep them mobile and active. The firm footing upon which we stand, and upon which we move forward, is nothing less than the gospel of peace. When Paul used this illustration of being shod with the equip-ment of the gospel of peace he probably had in his mind the words from Isaiah 52:7, 'How beautiful upon the mountains are the feet of him who brings good tidings, who publishes peace . . . .' There is a reference to this in Romans 10:14-15, and this passage suggests an urgency in sharing the good news with others. As we 'put on' this part of the armour, then, we are not only giving our-selves a firm foundation, but we are announcing our will-ingness, even our eagerness, to be bearers of the good news of Jesus Christ to others, to be peacemakers between man and man or between man and God.

This is no easy option. I remember a very well-known Lydia leader coming to this point of the preparation one day, at a conference, and saying firmly, 'Shoes, please, not carpet slippers!' No comfortable rejoicing by our own firesides for us! We are accepting the fact that, as Christians, we are on active service, ready to be bearers and doers of the word anywhere at any time at God's command.

The shield of faith

A most important piece of armour this! 'Above all,' says Paul, 'taking the shield of faith' (Eph 6:16). This provides overall protection against anything and everything with which Satan may attack us – all his 'fiery darts', in fact. The devil is the great scoffer, the great perverter and distorter of truth. Ridicule, doubt and fear are only some of his 'darts'. But we live by faith in the Son of God (Gal 2:20), and we need to be steeped in all the promises of God, remembering that 'he who promised is faithful' (Heb 10:23). Earlier in our preparation we mentioned the sin of unbelief; was this, I wonder, what the writer of Hebrews had in mind when he spoke of 'the sin which doth so easily beset us' (Heb 12:1 AV)? 'What on earth am *I* doing here?' you may ask yourself. 'God doesn't want *me*. How can my prayer be of any use? We are spending time here which might more profitably have been spent doing something useful. Better to go and visit someone; write a letter; organize a protest; almost anything is better than sitting around here all day praying!'

Oh, the craftiness of it! These and many other worse doubts and fears will creep up on us if we are not watchful. You may well like to think at this point of the devil, as Peter described him, prowling up and down like a hungry lion. But 'Resist him, firm in your faith,' says Peter (1 Pet 5:9). Turn to Jesus, then, and allow him to make your faith perfect (Heb 12:2), and take hold of this mighty shield with which you will be able not just to ward off, but to put out *all* the fiery darts of the evil one.

The helmet of salvation

When we speak of salvation we think immediately of that which has been done for us upon the cross by Jesus. He has paid the price for the sin of the whole world – we have been redeemed, 'bought back' from the power of the devil (Heb 2:14-15). Looking up the meaning and origin of the word 'salvation' I find among the roots from which it stems such words as: 'cure', 'recovery', 'redemption', 'remedy', 'rescue' and 'welfare'. It is said to mean the action or result of deliverance or preservation from danger or disease. It implies safety, health and prosperity.

All the words I have just quoted can be applied to Christ's total work of salvation, and we need to bear in mind that our physical, as well as our spiritual well-being is in his hands. Remember that God has provided us with every protection against the attacks of the devil, and do not underestimate the determination of Satan to undermine and prevent the work of God's servants by any means at his disposal. If he cannot get at us with his lies and deceptions, or lure us away with worldly thoughts and desires, he may well attack us physically.

John Wesley told how he often felt ill before preaching, but once he got going the sickness would disappear. We need to be sure that tiredness, headaches, etc, are not allowed to hinder our prayer. They may be due to a spirit of heaviness, or depression, and we should exercise our authority over them. (Of course, they may be due to lack of sleep, in which case we must take the appropriate action!) There are all kinds of accidents and calamities which may befall us, not least upon the roads as we journey to and from our meeting place. Sometimes God in-

tervenes miraculously to defend his servants, but in our
ordinary day-to-day affairs what is necessary is that our
minds should be so consecrated to him that the mislead-
ing and damaging thoughts and suggestions of the enemy
can find no resting place there. If our minds are under
God's protection and open to his direction, he will tell us
what to do in every situation, and thus we shall pass
safely through any and every hazard which Satan may
contrive to put in our way. Take the helmet of salvation,
therefore, and avail yourself of *all* that Christ offers in
his saving work, asking him as you do so to protect you
from accident, sickness, tiredness, and all the damaging thoughts of the evil one, and to keep your mind
open and alert, especially in this time of prayer, to
receive his thoughts and directions only.

The sword of the Spirit, which is the word of God

'For the word of God is living and active, sharper than
any two-edged sword, piercing to the division of soul and
spirit, of joints and marrow, and discerning the thoughts
and intentions of the heart' (Heb 4:12-13). We are thinking here of Scripture, and of the word which the Holy
Spirit will bring to our minds at the appropriate moment.
What power there is in the word of God! It shares the
qualities of God himself, being alive, full of activity and
might to fulfil his purposes. God himself is active in his
word, so that properly used, under the direction of the
Holy Spirit, it can never be ineffective (Is 55:11). Inevitably either salvation or judgement results. See how
swiftly and deftly it goes to the very heart of a matter,
how it penetrates to the very deepest places of our being,
bringing to light the true nature of the thoughts hidden
therein. Face to face with the word of God we are face to
face with God himself, from whom nothing is hidden and
who alone judges all men and all things.

This, then, is the sword of the Spirit, through which

God will often speak, giving us understanding and discernment concerning the matters for which we are praying and with which we shall confront the hosts of the enemy.

See how Jesus 'full of the Holy Spirit' responded to Satan's cunning with appropriate words of Scripture, to which the devil had no answer and against which he was powerless (Lk 4:1-13). It is good to keep this 'sword' sharp and ready for use at any time by making sure that we have a good knowledge of the Scriptures for the Holy Spirit to draw on, and that we regularly meditate upon them, so that our intercessions may be focused upon the covenanted promises of God. However, you cannot always remember everything, so always have your Bible with you and a concordance conveniently at hand, so that a reference or verse half remembered may quickly be found. Once again let me say that there is nothing 'unspiritual' about being efficient, but it would be very 'unspiritual' indeed to miss the direction of the Holy Spirit through your inability to follow up a verse or a reference which he has called to mind!

Exercise your authority over the enemy

In spiritual warfare we shall be going into enemy territory, and in this kind of activity we are to 'first bind the strong man' (Mt 12:29). Satan is not going to just open the door and let us in, but Jesus has given us authority over Satan (see Mt 18:18 and Lk 10:19) and it is up to us to exercise it. So now let the leader, or someone else if this has been previously arranged, do this simply, in the following manner: 'Satan, in the name of Jesus and with his authority, we bind you and all principalities and powers who would seek to come against us and hinder our prayer, and we make you totally ineffective.' It is good to declare again the lordship of Jesus over your gathering and to pray in tongues for a few moments, if the Holy Spirit moves you to do so.

Ask for the fear of God to come upon you

What we are asking for here is *holy* fear, sometimes called awe (Is 11:2-3), so that in God's presence we shall not turn aside from anything he reveals to us, nor hold back anything he brings to mind through fear of being wrong, however small or irrelevant it may seem. It may be a picture, a tongue or an interpretation, a verse of Scripture, a word of knowledge or prophecy, and we soon learn, sometimes to our surprise in the beginning, that we all have the same Spirit within us, as we share these things and begin to discern the overall direction that he is giving us together. 'The fear of the Lord is the beginning of wisdom; a good understanding have all those who practise it' (Ps 111:10). A very pertinent verse for intercessors!

Worship God and praise him

'Ah Lord God! It is thou who has made the heavens and the earth by thy great power and by thy outstretched arm! Nothing is too hard for thee . . . O great and mighty God whose name is the Lord of hosts, great in counsel and mighty in deed' (Jer 32:17-20). 'God so loved the world that he gave his only Son, that whoever believes in him should not perish but have eternal life' (Jn 3:16).

We have 'come in' to God to make ourselves available to him and to allow him to make us ready to 'go out' into spiritual warfare in his name. Now is the time to worship him and to praise him for who he is, for what he has done and is doing. You will find your own acclamations coming to mind as you praise him in words and in song, however the Spirit moves. The psalmist speaks of God as being 'enthroned' on the praises of his people (Ps 22:3), or 'inhabiting' their praises (AV), and in this time of relaxed worship and praise we do indeed enthrone him in our midst. We exalt him! Relax and rejoice in his presence, and the leader will be sensitive to the Holy Spirit's direction as to when this time is to lead into the time of intercession. Then she will invite the group to be silent for a while, to listen to God.

5

'Whatever You Ask in My Name'

The simple dictionary definition of the phrase 'in the name of . . .' is 'with the authority of . . .' and 'on behalf of . . .' which is said to mean 'in the interests of . . .' or 'for the sake of . . .'. These definitions carry the implication that what is being said or done is in accordance with the wishes of the person whose name is being used. The person speaking or acting is doing so as though he were that other person. We tend to think of someone's name as a kind of label which enables us to identify one person from another, in speech or in writing, but in the Bible the name and the person are much more closely equated. The name denotes the active presence of the person in the fullest sense of all his characteristics (see 1 Kings 18:24ff, Elijah's contest of 'names'), and is also equated with personal reputation, especially where God is asked, or said, to act 'for his name's sake' (Ps 79:9 and Ezek 36:21-23). 'Where his name is implicated he is personally involved, and will take personal action' (*New Bible Dictionary,* page 863).

To do something in the name of someone else is a big responsibility anyway, but with the biblical understanding of 'name' in mind, to ask something 'in the name of Jesus' becomes very significant indeed. The name of Jesus is not merely a mark of approval to be stamped at the bottom of our petitions. We are to use it when, with his authority, we ask those things which he would ask; those things which are in accordance with his will and character.

Now, as intercessors, we begin to understand the need for our preparation; it is in order to focus our attention upon *God,* so that the directions we receive in this time of waiting upon him may be those of his Holy Spirit and not merely 'impressions' from the human spirit.

So how are we to know that it *is* God directing us? The simple answer is first that we must trust him – and ourselves – and then we have an absolutely reliable criterion in Scripture and in the agreed witness of the church. God never contradicts himself and will not direct us in any way contrary to his word, and his revelation of himself in Christ Jesus, nor to his consistent direction of his people through the ages. Therefore, if we are singlemindedly intent upon serving him by means of our prayer, if we have truly consecrated our minds and our wills to him and meditated much and prayerfully upon his word, we must proceed in faith, in the confident expectation that he will lead us and teach us. Otherwise we are back to the wind-tossed waves and the unstable man of James 1:6-8.

Now is the time for the leader of the group to ask the Holy Spirit for direction as to what or who to pray for, and remember that in prayer there are no boundaries, geographical or otherwise, to limit what he may bring before you.

The Holy Spirit moves
man to discover man;
his inspiration proves
more than the heart can span.
Each listening heart is led to find
the will of God for all mankind.

Frederik Herman Kaan, from *Pilgrim Praise,* © Stainer & Bell Ltd 1968.

Wait in silence, then allow him to speak to each one of you. Once again, it is no good being vague and wishy-washy with God. He will have something specific to say to you collectively, so have your notebooks and pens at the ready before you begin so that you may now write down what he says to you individually in order to be able to share it competently when the time comes. It is important not to move on from this stage until everyone is ready – look up when you are, so that the leader will know, and then she can encourage and lead the sharing of what has been given. Sometimes a very clear and definite direction will emerge immediately, sometimes there may be a number of different, apparently unrelated matters. It may be possible to see straight away that God is giving you several different things to pray about during the course of your time of intercession, in which case the next step is to ask him which you are to take first. Or it may be necessary to wait upon him again to see how the various matters he has brought to mind relate together, and to see his overall plan.

On one occasion, I remember, the group were sharing what he had given in the time of listening and, as each one shared, it was immediately obvious that he was giving us direction to pray for the families of our nation. There was a particular reference to some of the things in our national life which currently undermine the stability of our families. The emphasis was upon the fathers, who so often these days are either unwilling or unable to fulfil their proper role as head of the family under Christ. The youngest and newest member of the group, who had never shared in this way before, was somewhat uncertain when her turn came, because she felt led to pray for the students at our university, especially the young men, and she couldn't see what this had to do with what the rest of us were saying. We encouraged her, and then as we asked God about it we understood that these students were fathers of the future and, hopefully, some of them would become articulate and influential members of society. With this additional piece of direction our prayer quickly became very specific and relevant.

Having ascertained what God wants us to pray about, we now have to ask him *how,* and it may be necessary to alternate between some short times of silence and sharing in order to do this, and this is where the contents and abilities of our consecrated minds are used by God. As people who are concerned to intercede for those around us, for the local situation, for the nation as a whole, and for nations worldwide, we will have been watching and reading the news and acquainting ourselves with what goes on in our own locality and further afield. We cannot all keep in touch with everything, because we have finite minds. However, every member of the group will have something to contribute to the general pool of knowledge and experience upon which the Holy Spirit may now draw. Although we have set aside our own thoughts and opinions in order to receive his, we do not come to prayer empty-minded, like some spiritual Mother Hubbard. Rather we have placed at his disposal all that we have and are, and can be assured he will use it. This, too, is where we see the importance of having kept our 'swords' sharp by constant and regular reading and meditating upon the Scriptures, for as we now hold before God the particular matter about which he is directing us to pray, he will often use his word to bring understanding and insight into a situation or a need, and with Scripture we may confront the enemy, as Jesus did.

Often, too, as we hold before him a person or a situation, we experience that insight which comes not from our own experience or understanding, but directly from the Holy Spirit – the word of knowledge as it is called.

All that God gives to us, while we seek direction, we must gently share with one another, the leader being sensitive to when it is appropriate to be silent and listen to God, and when to speak and share. Let that holy fear be upon us, that we hold nothing back, and, perhaps again to our surprise at first, a definite strategy of prayer will emerge and we shall see how we are to pray. There is really only one effective way of learning how to seek and obtain God's direction in prayer in this way, and that is to get on and do it! A thousand words of mine, or anyone else's, will never substitute for one half-hour of actual experience.

I said that we should see what to ask for *or do*. Sometimes the Holy Spirit will move us to ask him for something, for his intervention and action in a matter, for the ministry of angels, for healing, and so on. But often he will require us to *do* something. Perhaps you are to proclaim the lordship of Jesus in a particular situation – if so, do it with confidence, in word and in song, for as long as the Spirit moves you. Or it may be that you are again to exercise the authority you have over the powers of darkness. In our preparation we bound Satan and his minions, rendering them powerless over our time of intercession, but we may now have to bind them specifically with regard to certain circumstances. This may be done very simply and will have the effect of keeping the powers of darkness at bay and preventing them from spreading or continuing their influence. We may now invite the Holy Spirit into the situation, so that he, not they, may influence and direct what is happening. This kind of intercessory activity is often directed by the Holy Spirit as a preparation and support for some actual physical intervention or activity which he has assigned to someone else, and we shall be looking at this again a little later on.

There are several ways in which God may speak to us in these times. As well as through Scripture and the word of knowledge, or revelation, which we have already mentioned, he may use prophecy, or tongues and interpretation, or one of us may have a 'prayer picture', a visual aid from the Lord, perhaps not only to direct but also to encourage us with a glimpse of what is being accomplished in the spiritual realm.

There are also many different ways in which we may express our prayer. As a child I learnt to kneel down, put my hands together, close my eyes, and speak to God, and I still pray like that, but since I have learnt to allow the Holy Spirit to direct me I have discovered that I can also use my body as a vehicle for prayer; I can weep, sigh, prostrate myself, or even move and dance, to give expression to what he is impressing upon my heart and soul. In the last part of this book we shall be looking more closely at some of these ways of praying. The important thing is to learn together to be free in the Spirit, in worship and intercession, to give the fullest expression, be it in movement or in stillness, in sound or in silence, to whatever he gives us.

Ask – declare – proclaim – bind and loose, with confidence and authority. 'Whatever he says – do it!'

Continue listening, sharing and praying until you are sure you have fulfilled all that God requires of you concerning that topic. The leader has a responsibility to see that nobody leads off onto something else. If someone does, she must gently bring them back to the matter in hand until all are agreed that there is no more to be done – except to praise God and thank him. Offer your thanksgiving to him now for all that he has begun to do and will continue to do. 'And this is the confidence which we have in him, that if we ask anything according to his will he hears us. And if we know that he hears us in whatever we ask, we know that we have obtained the requests made of him' (1 Jn 5:14-15).

Now you are ready to turn to other matters, if there are any, and take them one by one in the same manner, always listening for God's direction and patiently fulfilling all that he gives you before moving on to something else. Thus your prayer on any topic will be complete for this time together, though in some cases you may be aware of the need for persistent, prevailing prayer which will continue in your heart and in your own private time with the Lord; and it may be that he will call the group back to this topic on another occasion.

When all has been done as the Lord has directed, come to a closing time of praise and worship and acclamation. 'Hell's foundations quiver at the shout of praise . . . .'

Perhaps you will be wondering, 'Did we get it right?' Well, we're not perfect – indeed in this life we have only very partial understanding and even prophecy and knowledge are imperfect (1 Cor: 13:8-12), but I believe God 'edits' and uses even our mistakes if we have done all in a spirit of humble obedience, for who among us can say we have always perfectly understood and obeyed? I love the words of St Teresa of Avila, 'God does not require a perfect work, but *infinite desire.*' It is that infinite desire which is so precious to the heart of God and which, joined to faith in him, enables us to move mountains and pull down strongholds.

So praise him! Worship him! And rest content. Go home rejoicing and keep all these things in your heart. What is given to us by God in the place of prayer is a matter between him and us and should never be lightly shared and discussed with others. The Lord who 'sees in secret' knows, and that is enough.

But is this all? What about the answers to our prayer? How shall we know what happened? We live in a world of instant everything, from coffee to communications. Ever since Alexander Graham Bell invented the telephone and Marconi received the first transatlantic radio signal, we have become more and more conditioned to experiencing instant reaction and response. Now the touch of a button brings a picture to our television screen and events on the other side of the world are immediately visible in our sitting rooms. We take all this for granted and expect it as our right, but in prayer things are a little different.

It is certainly true that God always responds instantly, and effectively, to our prayer, and when, at his direction, we have bound Satan, proclaimed the lordship of Jesus, declared freedom to someone in bondage, or whatever, there is immediate reaction in the spiritual realms and something begins to happen straight away. However, unlike the case of the television screen, there may be no immediate, tangible evidence that something has happened. Sometimes, to be sure, we shall see at once the result of our prayer, right there before our eyes; or later that day, or the next day, something will happen which is clearly the answer to and the result of our prayer. At such a time it is easy to be joyful and to praise God for his goodness. Such times are a wonderful encouragement and we do well to be glad in them and to give God the glory. But we should be giving him the glory and rejoicing anyway, even when the visible signs of victorious prayer are delayed, perhaps for many weeks or months, if indeed we ever receive them at all. Some people, I know, find this lack of tangible proof disappointing, and difficult to accept, but here we are touching again on the deep mystery of prayer which I mentioned in chapter 1. We must come to terms with this if we are to be faithful, persistent and effective intercessors.

As we learn to consecrate our minds and wills to God, making ourselves available to him for this work of intercession, and trusting the direction of his Holy Spirit in our prayer, he will give us insight into events and circumstances far removed from our own actual experience – even in distant lands – as well as into situations close at hand. It follows, inevitably, that we may never know what has happened in every case. All we shall have is faith, 'the evidence of things not seen' (Heb 11:1 AV), and even when we do actually see the desired result come to pass – for example, concerning national matters – we shall never be able to declare, 'We did that. We prayed and that happened.' Who knows, except God alone, how many other people had been praying about that same thing at his direction? And the mystery of just how he has used our own particular prayer in bringing about his purposes is not, I think, to be made known to us in this life.

Intercession is very much a business for adult, mature Christians, and I don't necessarily mean those who are advanced in years, or even those who have been Christians for a long time, but rather those who have been weaned from the milk of their spiritual childhood onto the solid food of the mature (see Heb 5:13-14). If, like babies, we are still looking for the easily digestible 'milk' of instant proof and evidence, then we are not yet fully grown and strong enough for the mature work of spiritual warfare. Once weaned, however, God will give us, by his Holy Spirit, the 'solid food' of deep peace and assurance that we have been co-operating with him in his divine purposes.

And lest anyone should think that what I have just said savours of spiritual arrogance, let me refer you to the words of Jesus, when he set a small child before his disciples, 'Whoever humbles himself like this child, he is the greatest in the kingdom of heaven' (Mt 18:4). To be humble is, among other things, to be teachable, and it is in childlike, teachable humility that our spiritual maturity is born.

Another matter which sometimes disturbs and alas even divides those who are called to pray is the need for action. Surely we should be ready to be the answer, or part of the answer, to our own prayers? Yes, *if God says so*. During our preparation time, when we 'put on' the shoes of the gospel of peace, we acknowledged our readiness to be bearers and doers of the word anywhere, at any time, *at God's command*. It may well be that sometimes prayer should be followed by Spirit-controlled and directed action, but only if we are certain and agreed that this really is what he is saying. Some people, I know, feel that prayer inevitably moves into action, but I venture to suggest that this can be, if we are not on our guard, one of the enemy's subtlest and most effective red herrings. This is especially so as it can quickly bring people under condemnation and into the bondage of guilt if they find themselves unable, because of their circumstances, to enter into the kind of activity which suddenly seems to be required of them.

Most of us at some time or other will be moved by the Holy Spirit to take action of some kind, perhaps writing a letter to our MP or something similar, but I have known people to be thoroughly disconcerted and even discouraged from prayer, by the pressure put upon them by well-meaning, enthusiastic but misdirected friends. If God directs you to act, then act. If he does not, then don't, and do not have any doubt whatsoever in your mind that you have fulfilled your part in his purposes by praying, as you have done, at his direction. We must understand that prayer is of itself a divinely appointed and effective *work,* and it is a great mistake for those who 'do' to think that everyone else should be 'doing' something too. Indeed, very often it is only because of the faithful, secret work of the pray-ers that the do-ers are enabled to be effective anyway. Paul often asked his fellow Christians to *pray* for him in order that he might *do* his job more effectively. 'Pray at all times . . . for all the saints, and also for me, that utterance may be given me in opening my mouth boldly to proclaim the mystery of the gospel' (Eph 6:18-19).

In the first chapter I spoke of the intercessors in military terms as being something like the S.A.S., whose job it is to go behind the enemy lines secretly and to undermine and weaken their positions, in preparation for the rest of the force to come in. The work my son-in-law does for the Prison Fellowship, and his ministry in other connections also, has led him into difficult and sometimes potentially dangerous situations. He likens the intercessors to the artillery, whose consistent and persistent barrage (of prayer) opens up the way for people like himself to go in and do their work, and gives them protection while they do it.

I read some years ago of a convent in London, where the nuns take it in turns to pray throughout the night for those desperate, needy, or evil people who inhabit the city's darkness and go about their business under its cover, and for those who go out to find them and minister to them, bringing at least some of them into the Light of lights. The nuns themselves don't go out, but who would question the rightness of their sole preoccupation with prayer? Who knows what enabling power has been released through their faithfulness to their vocation to *pray?* There are many people, especially women, whose personal circumstances preclude any apparent involvement in the issues of the day, who are yet enabled to play a glorious part in the total work of the church through this powerful ministry of intercession.

There are two things of which I have become absolutely certain since I embarked upon this adventure of prayer.

The first is that prayer is the means by which Almighty God has chosen to release power into the world through the church. It is meant to be the very life blood of all our activity and endeavour, bringing down blessing from heaven. This is the means by which God heals, cleanses, transforms and renews, and without it the body of Christ on earth is rendered anaemic, weak and ineffective. The fact that he has chosen to work in this way is a humbling mystery to us all.

The second thing is that the kind of sacrificial, effective, availing prayer to which God calls us all, is dependent upon our life. 'It is the life that prays.' God has given us certain very clear promises concerning prayer: 'Whatever you ask in my name, I will do it' (Jn 14:13). 'Whatever you bind on earth shall be bound in heaven, and whatever you loose on earth shall be loosed in heaven . . . if two of you agree on earth . . . it will be done for them by my Father in heaven' (Mt 18:18-19). 'Whatever you ask in prayer, believe that you receive it, and you will' (Mk 11:24). But with these wonderful promises goes a very important condition: 'If you abide in me and my words abide in you, ask whatever you will, and it shall be done for you. By this my Father is glorified, that you bear much fruit' (Jn 15:7-8). 'As the branch cannot bear fruit by itself, unless it abides in the vine, neither can you, unless you abide in me' (Jn 15:4).

These great truths apply whether we meet to pray in groups or pray alone, or whatever God asks us to do for him. Our prayer will be 'fruitless' unless we are grafted and rooted in the Vine, daily drawing up the precious, life-giving sap of his Holy Spirit. We may never be able to weigh and measure the 'fruit' of our prayer, but the life that is joined to Christ, as much a part of him as the branch is of the vine, will bear an abundance of fruit to the glory of the Father.

6

Fellow Workers in the Truth

In all that I have said so far the emphasis has been on group intercession. Certainly to be part of a group and belonging to a fellowship of intercessors has its benefits, as we have seen from the way the Lydia Fellowship operates, but whatever your circumstances, and whether you pray alone or with others, the principles remain the same. All that I have said about preparation and waiting on the Lord for his directions may be applied effectively to the lone intercessor, though the benefit of sharing and agreement is lost, and I must confess it is easier when there are two or three together.

Now I am not suggesting that we cannot *pray* without first making the kind of preparation I have described. That would be absurd! Ever since the veil of the temple was torn in two from the top to the bottom we have had free and unimpeded access to the Father. Jesus himself said, 'I do not say to you that I will pray the Father for you; for the Father himself loves you' (Jn 16:26-27). We can come to him freely, with confidence as well as with awe and wonder, but in intercession we are *going out*, spiritually, and we should take advantage of everything that God provides, both in terms of spiritual equipment and by way of the fellowship and encouragement of other intercessors.

At this point it is good to remind ourselves that an army consists of much more than just the S.A.S. and the artillery, important though they are. The whole church is the 'mighty army' of God, and one of the vital necessities in any campaign is communication. None of us may be able to see the complete campaign as God sees it, but we do need to see our targets and to have information upon which the Holy Spirit may draw as he directs us in prayer. No one intercessor can be fully informed about every-thing, and even a group with the combined knowledge of all its members cannot hope to keep in touch with all that is going on. One advantage, therefore, of the larger fellow-ship, is being able to draw on a much bigger pool of information, and to circulate this information to its members. This applies locally as well as nationally. Those who have the opportunity or special call to follow what is going on in, for example, parliament, or local government affairs, are able to contribute their know-ledge to the common pool. In this way important matters affecting our national life at every level can be made known, and together we shall be fulfilling that very im-portant part of our calling – to be watchmen.

We shall all, of course, be playing our own part in this, by reading the newspapers and watching or listening to the news. But the other vital part of our communications system is to be in touch with the other 'units' of the army, the experts in the field. All Christians are called to pray. For us, as intercessors, this is a special responsi-bility, a specialized ministry, complementary to the specialized ministries of others.

In these times God has been raising up wonderful people and effective organizations to be watchmen and workers for him, in specific areas of national and inter-national life. We need each other. They need us to go before them, weakening the enemy, making a way for them, and supporting them constantly while they work.

We need them; we need the dedicated, tireless work they do – each in his own sphere – investigating, keeping watch, uncovering the hidden works of darkness, petitioning, campaigning, ministering. They need to know that we are with them, that we are praying with them and for them, and we need from them information about specific needs and concerns, so that when God directs our attention and our intercessory activity to any particular zone of the battle, our prayer may be pertinent. It may be, too, that God will give an individual or a group a special responsibility over a period of time, to pray for one particular concern, and they will find great encouragement and assistance from being in touch with those whose special area of work that is.

We are all in this together, and it is through this sharing of information that we are able to take part in joint prayer campaigns, at the direction of the Holy Spirit. Ours and other nations need the activities of intercessors and Christian workers as never before.

Christians, and men and women of goodwill everywhere, are deeply disturbed at the breakdown of marriages and the consequent disruption of family life. They are concerned over the spiritual and moral corruption of the young – and the not so young, come to that – and over many other issues, some of which I mentioned in the first chapter.

In recent years proposed legislation to make divorce even easier and quicker has been seen as yet another threat to the stability of family life. The crime figures for 1981 showed that 54% of convictions and cautions were for offences committed by people aged between ten and twenty-one, and that almost one third were under seventeen. The use of human embryos for experimental purposes; the new practice of surrogate motherhood; and the need to find a realistic solution to the problem of R18 videos (the 'nasties') are matters which have caused great anxiety in parliament and in the nation.

On the positive side, in December 1983 the Westminster City Council turned down all but six out of twenty-one applications for licensed sex shops, and the Greater London Council relicensed only three out of eighty Soho sex cinemas. I also know that nearer to my own home a City Council has decided that 'nil' is the appropriate number of sex shops for their city, and this has been the case in a good number of localities.

All these parliamentary debates and committee reports seem so complicated, and sometimes so dull and difficult to follow, that maybe some of us would be tempted to bypass them, if we were not made aware of what they represent in terms of potential and actual human degradation and misery. In many homes today young children watch violent and pornographic videos with the knowledge and consent of their parents – material that should never be available to them. What a state of affairs! How should I pray? How should you pray? We need all the help and guidance we can get.

Praise God for all those wonderful people who have responded to his call to be watchmen over our nation in very specific ways. Some of them, like Mrs Mary Whitehouse, have been pilloried for the stand they have taken. All of them work hard and sacrificially. We are all in this together.

I give here the names and addresses of just some of these organizations, with a brief note of what they cover. Some of you may already be aware of their work, and in touch with them, but for some readers this may be a helpful introduction. I do realize that there are other organizations which I am not able to include in this short list.

As I mention them I am aware of all the individual Christians – 'fellow workers in the truth' – represented by these names, and I am grateful for the privilege of being able to 'render service' to them by supporting them in prayer (see 3 Jn 5, 8).

CARE Trust

(Christian Action Research and Education) 21a Down Street, London W1Y 7DN.

This is a registered charity supporting Christian standards in society and believes that:

1. God cares about the state of our nation as he witnesses a steady erosion of moral and Christian values.

2. Rulers of every nation will one day have to give an account to God for the way they have governed. In a democracy we all share in this responsibility.

This trust has been set up to assist Christians to play their part in influencing the quality of our national life. In particular it promotes the values of individual human worth and family relationships as taught in the Bible.

It undertakes research into those trends in society which seriously affect human worth and family relationships. It is engaged in the education of people about these developments, giving positive Christian teaching, with the intention of encouraging Christian action to support what is good and to oppose what is harmful.

Against the background of increasing marriage and family breakdown, CARE Trust is committed to involving as many Christians as possible in the care and protection of the unborn, the young, marriages and families under strain, the handicapped and the elderly.

CARE Campaigns

Also at 21a Down Street, London W1Y 7DN.

A non-charitable body committed to the principle that law and public policy in our country should be in harmony with basic Christian principles.

The law forbids registered charities (such as CARE Trust) to lobby politically with a view to law change.

Therefore CARE Campaigns has been set up as a sister, but separate, organization, working to see law and public policy in our country brought into harmony with biblical principles.

National Viewers and Listeners Association

Ardleigh, Colchester, Essex CO7 7RH.
This organization believes:

1. That Christian values are basic to the health and wellbeing of our nation and therefore calls on the broadcasting authorities to reverse the current humanist approach to social, religious and personal issues.

2. That the broadcasting authorities should fulfil their legal obligations to ensure 'that nothing is included in the programmes which offends against good taste or decency or is likely to encourage or incite to crime or lead to disorder or to be offensive to public feeling' and 'that the programmes maintain a proper balance' (from the Television Act 1954 and Broadcasting Act 1981).

3. That violence on television contributes significantly to the increase of violence in society and should be curtailed.

4. That the use of swearing and blasphemy are destructive of our culture and our faith, and that the broadcasting authorities are remiss in allowing it.

5. That sexual innuendo and explicit sex trivialize and cheapen human relationships and undermine marriage and family life.

6. That the media are indivisible and that the quality of film, theatre and publishing inevitably affects broadcasting standards.

Its aims are:

1. To encourage viewers and listeners to react effectively to programme content.

2. To stimulate public and parliamentary discussion on the effects of broadcasting on the individual, the family

and society.

3. To secure effective legislation to control obscenity and pornography in the media – including broadcasting.

The Trinity Trust

57 Duke Street, Mayfair, London W1M 5DH.

The Trinity Trust was established in 1980 to provide support and encouragement to the churches by enabling professionally made educational material, explaining the Christian faith, to be made available through the various media. It recognizes that we must use the most modern facilities available in communicating our Christian faith.

Trinity Video

Grafton Place, Worthing, West Sussex BN11 1QX.

Created and owned by Trinity Trust, the aims of Trinity Video are:

1. To encourage Christians to use video to share the Christian faith.

2. To make trustworthy programming generally available, which does not rely upon sexual exploitation, gratuitous violence or profanity, but offers a high standard of entertainment and artistic integrity.

Prison Fellowship

(Formerly known as Prison Christian Fellowship) P.O. Box 263, London SW1.

Prison Christian Fellowship was launched in Britain in March 1979, following a series of conferences and much prayer. Its name is being changed to Prison Fellowship to fit in with the worldwide movement. Its aim is to build bridges of love and practical care between local churches of all denominations and the barren hopelessness of the prisoner's life.

Its method is to draw together and enable individuals with varying skills and experiences to share the message of Jesus Christ to all who are in prison. This is done by:

Praying with and for prison chaplains, volunteers and organizations already working with prisoners.

Teaching Christian truths through Bible seminars conducted in prisons.

Building up the body of Christ within the prisons.

Linking prisoners and their families in need with caring Christians.

Helping ex-prisoners find accommodation and employment.

Prison Fellowship have prayer groups in many places, particularly near to our penal institutions. Intercessors with a special call to pray concerning the work with prisoners may like to join one of these.

If you are a new intercessor, or at present praying alone, and would like to join or be in touch with others, one of the following may be of help to you:

The Lydia Fellowship

This consists of many small groups of women joined together in the way described in chapter 2. Write for information leaflets and the name and address of the nearest area leader to: Mrs C. Leage, 121 Davey Drive, Brighton, Sussex BN1 7BF.

Intercessors For Britain

At the time of writing IFB has about 3,000 members. Just under half of these are 'lone' intercessors and just over half pray in groups of various sizes. The original aim was to establish a chain of intercession covering every day of the week, and people covenant, for a year at a time, to cover a certain period each week in the way best suited to their circumstances. Bulletins are sent to every member bi-monthly. Write for information to: Intercessors for Britain, 16 Orchard Road, Moreton, Merseyside.

Other countries have adopted this idea and have their own independent intercessory movements, which do have links between them, and have international conferences every two years. About thirty countries are involved in this way.

Prayer for Israel

P.O. Box 1, Golant, Cornwall.
For those with a special interest in, and desire to pray for Israel and the scattered Jewish people.

Maranatha News Sheet

3 Kipling Road, Stratford upon Avon, Warks.
This is an information sheet circulated to individuals and prayer groups on request, giving various topics for prayer – mainly selected from items reported in the press and media. Write to Sister Madge Turnbull.

All the foregoing information has been given to me by the organizations concerned, or has been taken, with permission, from their own introductory leaflets. More details can be obtained from the addresses given.

> I urge that petitions, prayers, requests, and thanksgivings be offered to God for all people; for kings and all others who are in authority, that we may live a quiet and peaceful life with all reverence towards God and with proper conduct. This is good and it pleases God our Saviour, who wants everyone to be saved and to come to know the truth (1 Tim 2:1-4 GNB).

PART TWO

What Happens When We Say Yes

Jesus is changing me,
Jesus is changing me,
The work of the Refiner's fire.
To be as pure gold
In the house of the Lord,
To give right offerings to Him.

To Him I give all my love and praise,
With joy I draw near to Him.
The Sun of Righteousness rises
    over me
With healing in his wings.

Then shall the blessing of the Lord
    come down,
When we give all to Him,
And we shall go forth in holiness,
Delighting ourselves in God.

A. Huntley, © Thankyou Music 1978.

7

The Humble Heart – an Experience of Love

Lord, show me what it means to have a humble heart,
Lord, show me what it means to love the world like you.
Lord, show me what it means to give my life away.
Lord, show me what it means to love you more each day.

Mark Pendergrass, Sparrow Song/Candle Co. Music/World Artist Music Co. Inc/World Music (UK), a division of Word (UK) Ltd, Northbridge Rd, Berkhamsted, Herts HP4 1EH.

God's call comes to us just as we are, with all our sins, fears, doubts, anxieties – in all the frailty of our human nature. But whenever we say yes to God, whenever we give him our heart's unconditional response and surrender, he is able to begin his loving work of changing us, renewing us. Perhaps you are thinking that he has done great things in your life already. There is always more. As often as he calls you to some new venture, some new step of faith, he will want to continue his sovereign work in you, preparing and equipping you for what is to come. Because he is God, our loving Father, this changing, renewing and equipping, will be a work of love. He needs us to be 'as pure gold' in his house; to be fit for the work to which he has called us, and we need have no fear. There is no loss in this, only pure gain for us, even if some of the changing is painful at first.

I have called this chapter 'The Humble *Heart*' because when God calls us it is to the *heart* that he speaks. The heart is our point of contact with him. It is the centre of our emotions; the seat of our will. We like to think that we make decisions with our mind, but I would like to suggest that it is what we care about, our affections, and the attitude of our heart, which has the greatest effect upon how we *use* our minds and upon what we do. Therefore our heart is the place where decisions are made – good or bad – and it is from the heart that our response of love and faith flows. Or it is our heart which we 'harden' when we turn away and refuse to respond to God, or to our fellow men.

So then, God's call to us to be his intercessors is received, and our response begun, in our hearts. What will it mean to us, as intercessors, to make ourselves totally available to him? To come, just as we are, seeking nothing for ourselves, not knowing what to expect, but prepared to do and to be whatever he asks of us?

When we begin to glimpse the largeness, the comprehensiveness, of what it is God sets before us, we say, 'How can this be?' What kind of a heart can respond to such a call? Only a heart which is not puffed up with grand ideas of its own importance; only a heart which is prepared to learn; only a heart that is willing to trust.

Here we need to learn first the secret of true humility. God is inviting us to co-operate with him, to play a part in his eternal purposes for all mankind, and our immediate and instinctive cry is, 'How can this be? Lord, I am not worthy.' But look at Mary – the Mother of our Lord and a wonderful example of true humility – and learn from her. For the response of the truly humble heart takes a step beyond the recognition of its own unworthiness and says, 'Nevertheless, be it unto me according to thy word.' This is the kernel of true humility, the recognition not just that we are unworthy, but that *he is able*. The heart that stops short at 'Lord, I am not worthy' has not yet learnt to gaze into the Father's face with simple, uncomplicated trust, tranquil and quiet like a child in its mother's arms (Ps 131). Such a heart is still concerned with its own image, for it sees the possibility of failure, and draws back. The truly humble heart, on the other hand, looks beyond its own limitations to the omnipotence of the Father, and, being yielded to him, becomes one with him in love and trust, in purpose and achievement, for with God all things are possible.

'Lord, show me what it means to have a humble heart.'

When we have come to a proper recognition of our own inability and God's ability, then we are in a position to learn, and this means that we have to be content to start wherever our Teacher wants us to start, and to move at his pace. It will be no good setting our sights on great and mighty matters, on the burning issues of the day, unless and until he says so. We may long to see the mountains shake and strongholds come tumbling down, and so we shall. But at any given moment, no matter how long we have been intercessors, it has to be enough for us to receive direction from God in simple obedience and humility, and concern ourselves only with whatever he gives us, however lowly and unimportant it may seem.

'Lord, my heart has no lofty ambitions, my eyes do not look too high. I am not concerned with great affairs or marvels beyond my scope' (Ps 131 Jerusalem Bible).

Two or three years ago the Rev. Barry Kissel came to a Lydia Conference at Swanwick, and during our time there he gave a talk which had the same title as this chapter. Few of us who heard it will forget his little illustration of the steps going down. He told us how he had been speaking one day and had been saying that the Christian life was like a series of plateaux. There we are on one plateau and God asks us to do something else. 'Oh no, Lord,' we say, 'I couldn't possibly do that.' But the Lord encourages us, 'Come on, trust me,' and at last we allow the Holy Spirit to have his way, and God lifts us up onto a new plateau. Barry went on to say that after that talk a friend took him on one side and suggested that perhaps he had got it a bit wrong. 'It's not plateaux,' said his friend, 'but steps. Steps going *down*.' Jesus humbled himself. He laid aside his right of equality with God to become the servant of mankind. He made this amazing progression from heaven to earth, into the deep sufferings of mankind, and then lower still, down to the death on the cross. Steps going down. *Then* God raised him, exalted him, and gave him a name which is above every name.

So forget your lofty ambitions – even your lofty prayer ambitions! Take your eyes off the great affairs and marvels which are not your business. Humble yourself and become obedient. Only in this way will you begin to have a share in the eternal purposes of God.

'Lord, show me what it means to love the world like you.'

What a thing to ask, that we might love as God loves! Dare we pray that? Yet we must pray it, for essentially the call to intercede is the call to love, and to love, moreover, without any reserve, unconditionally and unilaterally. This is where the cost begins to tell, for love is nothing if not vulnerable, and to invite God to give you even a measure of his great love for the world is to invite suffering as well as joy. It is to open your heart to your brothers and sisters of every race, colour and creed, in every circumstance known to mankind, the lovely and the unlovely. It is to *feel with them* (and this is the true meaning of sympathy). It is to experience – as far as God gives you grace to do so – the joy, the pain, the anguish and the delight, of those of his children whom he lays particularly upon your heart in prayer. It is to take unto yourself something of his sorrow and compassion, and to yearn with him over the whole of travailing creation (Rom 8:22).

How great is the love of God! 'God so loved the world that he gave his only Son' (Jn 3:16). We cannot fully feel the depth, breadth and intensity of the love which dwells in the heart of God, but as we make ourselves unconditionally available to him he will draw us into an ever growing experience of his own all-embracing love for all mankind.

'If anyone says, "I love God," and hates his brother, he is a liar . . . and this commandment we have from him, that he who loves God should love his brother also' (1 Jn 4:20-21).

'Lord, who is my brother?'

Your brother is 'any man', your sister is 'any woman'.

He is the skinny baby in the arms of a despairing woman; he is also the trades unionist you cannot agree with and the politician whose attitude drives you frantic; your best friend and the lout on the corner of the street.

She is the Queen of England; the stripper; and the woman who perms your hair.

He is the Sikh; the Muslim and the atheist; the terrorist and the President of the United States.

She is your mother-in-law; Mother Teresa; and the girl down the road who just had an abortion.

He is 'any man'. She is 'any woman'.

And this love that we are to have is not an optional extra – it is a commandment (1 Jn 4:21; Jn 15:12, 17).

This is the love which is so important that Paul was moved to write that without it nothing we can do is of any value, and even with the gifts of the Holy Spirit – tongues, prophecy, knowledge and miraculous power – he reckoned himself as nothing without love (1 Cor 13). This is *agape*, the 'love of the undeserving', the love which God has for us, in that 'while we were yet sinners Christ died for us' (Rom 5:8), and which he pours into our hearts by the Holy Spirit (Rom 5:5). It is nothing less than God himself in our hearts through the indwelling of the Holy Spirit.

God *is* love (1 Jn 4:8).

'Lord, show me what it means to give my life away.'

It is this love which makes it possible for us to intercede and engage in spiritual warfare, and it is this love which sustains our prayer.

Love and warfare do not seem to go very well together, yet in this fight against the dark forces of evil, love is at once our motivating force and our most potent weapon. Love is the very opposite of all that motivates and arms the enemy. Pride, envy, malice, lust, greed, anger and impurity, are some of the characteristics of his motives and weapons. How shall we come against these things? This is a specially important question for women, for the whole concept of battle and warfare seems essentially unfeminine, but in this war 'the weapons of our warfare are not carnal [that is, the world's weapons], but mighty through God (2 Cor 10:4 AV), and 'God is love' (1 Jn 4:8). Among the characteristics of love are gentleness, patience, kindness, forbearance, goodness and faithfulness. Perhaps this is one reason why so many women are numbered among the mighty prayer warriors, that their very weakness allows them to be strong with his strength (2 Cor 12:10), a familiar paradox to Christians. Therefore, we can say at one and the same time, 'He trains my hands for war, so that my arms can bend a bow of bronze . . . thou didst make my assailants sink under me' (Ps 18:34, 39), and 'Behold, I am the handmaid of the Lord' (Lk 1:38), with all that familiar phrase implies of meekness, humility, and gentle, willing obedience.

It is God who gives us the victory, and because God is love it is love that conquers.

So give yourself in true humility to the whole world, looking with steadfast love and trust into the face of your Father. Recognize your own weakness, yes, but know that there are no boundaries or limitations to what can be achieved, not by might or by power, but by the Spirit of God (see Zech 4:6), by his tender, compassionate, mighty love.

> Lord, give me grace inside to have a humble heart.
> Lord, give me grace inside to love the world like you.
> Lord, give me grace inside to give my life away.
> Lord, give me grace inside to love you more each day.

Mark Pendergrass, Sparrow Song

8

Called to Be Holy –
Called to Be Free

Holiness and freedom go hand in hand.

Many years ago there was a popular song which proclaimed that love and marriage 'go together like a horse and carriage' and it went on to declare that 'you can't have one without the other'. Sadly we know this is not always true, but when it comes to holiness and freedom it *is* true. You can't have one without the other.

When I was a child I knew what holy people were. They were saints of the stained-glass variety, complete with haloes, and they got themselves into those pretty windows by going about in a solemn and suitably saintly manner, doing all kinds of good deeds – and preferably also a few miracles – and they never, ever, made a mistake, got cross, or said an unkind word.

However, I learnt in time that saints come, as they always have, in all shapes and sizes and under all manner of disguises. Some are quiet, studious and thoughtful; some are lively and hearty; many laugh a lot and make me laugh too; all have sinned; most have made fools of themselves at least once in a while, and none are even vaguely aware of their own saintliness. But they are all holy, and they are all free. In other words, saints are mostly *ordinary* people whose lives manifest that elusive quality which we call holiness.

Heaven help us when we become preoccupied with our own holiness! That is an insidious form of idolatory. But we do need to think about holiness, for that is what God requires of us – that we become holy in body, mind and spirit – and as intercessors we cannot enter into effective spiritual warfare against anything that has not been dealt with in our own lives.

'I appeal to you therefore, brethren,' says Paul, 'to present your bodies . . . holy and acceptable' (Rom 12:1). 'God's temple is holy, and that temple you are' (1 Cor 3:17).

Peter tells us that we are to be 'a holy priesthood' (1 Pet 2:5) and, speaking of what is to come he asks, 'What sort of persons ought you to be in lives of holiness and godliness?' (2 Pet 3:11).

Again and again we are exhorted to seek holiness.

'God has not called us for uncleanness, but in holiness,' and, 'whoever disregards this, disregards not man but God' (1 Thess 4:7-8).

'Put on the new nature . . . in true righteousness and holiness' (Eph 4:24).

'Let us cleanse ourselves from every defilement of body and spirit, and make holiness perfect in the fear of God' (2 Cor 7:1).

'Strive for . . . the holiness without which no one will see the Lord' (Heb 12:14).

And if we need any further exhortation we have our Lord's own unequivocal statement, 'You, therefore, must be perfect, as your heavenly Father is perfect' (Mt 5:48).

What then is holiness and why is it inextricably connected with freedom?

The word 'holy' shares the same root as 'whole', 'heal' and 'healthy', which is very interesting. The call to holiness is not a call to some kind of insipid pseudo-sanctity, in which we deny ourselves all the normal expressions of our humanity. Letting go of our own selfish desires is called for, yes, and very often costly sacrifice, but this is not to deny our humanness. We are called to be *whole,* and that means to be the fully rounded-out human beings God created us to be, in that state of life to which it has pleased him to call us. To be whole is to be complete, with nothing missing, broken or impaired. My dictionary defines something that is whole as being 'a unity, an undivided, unbroken individual entity with all parts duly proportioned, adjusted and interrelated; a complete system'. I think that just about sums it up! And health is said to be the *'normal* condition of mind or body [or spirit] in which all parts and faculties perform their functions duly, easily and satisfactorily' (italics mine). That's holiness! The seagull gliding effortlessly past the window, and the blue-tit who is currently surveying the nest box in our garden, glorify their Creator all the time, simply by being what he intends them to be. When we begin to function like that we begin to give glory to God. We begin to be holy.

At once it becomes apparent that a great deal of our striving is unnecessary, and very likely counterproductive. 'Let go and let God' was the very good advice given to me years ago by a very wise and holy man.

It also becomes apparent to most of us that we ourselves are not 'whole' and 'healthy' in the way I have described. We are not holy. We long to belong completely to God, to be devoted to him and set apart for his service, which is also part of the definition of 'holiness', yet somehow we are not free to be as we would like to be. Why not? What prevents us? What gets in our way?

Sin is the answer to those questions, as we all know. Mostly it is our own sin, but sometimes it is the inherited effect of the sin of someone else.

Now we come to the third of our words related to holy – 'heal'. In order to become holy, which is 'whole' and 'healthy', we need to be healed; to be restored to the completeness and the effectiveness of our God-given human nature.

All that we can say about sin, repentance, forgiveness and restoration is of course applicable and relevant to all Christians, and as intercessors we need especially to be able to hear God; to be in such close communication with him that his messages and directions get through to us unhindered. Nothing hinders communication with God like sin. To have unrepented sin in our lives is to have a fault on the line between us, and it has to be cleared before normal dialogue can be resumed. For most of us, most of the time, this means coming frequently to the foot of the cross, and quietly and simply confessing to God our current mistakes and failures and receiving the forgiveness and love which he is ever ready and waiting to bestow upon us – allowing him to fill us afresh with his Holy Spirit to strengthen us and lead us in the right way. Because Jesus Christ has taken our guilt upon him and paid the price for our sin, it really is that simple (see 1 Jn 1: 8-10).

Sometimes, however, it doesn't seem quite that simple. There may be a long-standing, deeply rooted sin, something that has really got hold of us, and we cannot but acknowledge our own responsibility for this state of affairs. It's not that there is one temptation which we are quite unable to resist, one sin which, try as we might, we commit time and time again, because 'God is faithful, and he will not let you be tempted beyond your strength, but with the temptation will also provide the way of escape, that you may be able to endure it' (1 Cor 10:13). Rather it is our own inclination to sin, our sin-full attitude, which is responsible, and this is why we find it so difficult to escape. It is not by chance that we talk about the 'slavery of sin'. By persisting in our sin, nurturing an affection for it even, and putting off the moment when we deal with it, we effectively sell ourselves into slavery. We are not free to serve God; we are bound, and therefore our growth and development as sons of God is stunted; we cease to be whole, healthy and holy.

Have you ever had a whitlow? Nasty things, whitlows. It may start off as a tiny abscess under or near your finger nail, and if you apply the right treatment quickly, you may save yourself a lot of misery, but if you neglect it, that little abscess will grow and develop until your whole finger is swollen and throbbing with pain, and quite useless. At that stage the measures required to deal with it may be quite drastic. This is the effect that sin has upon us. At first it may be only a 'finger' that is put out of action. Later it may be our whole being.

The appropriate treatment for sin is confession and a hearty repentance, which entails a change of attitude and the forgiveness of God. 'If we confess our sins, he is faithful and just, and will forgive our sins and cleanse us from all unrighteousness' (1 Jn 1:9). Remember that with the forgiveness comes also cleansing. 'The blood of Jesus . . . cleanses us from all sin' (1 Jn 1:7). Cleansed by that precious blood and reclothed in the righteousness of Jesus, we come before the throne of grace.

Charles Wesley, in one of his well known hymns, declared that his chains fell off, and that's just what it is like, but some people do seem to have a great deal of trouble disentangling themselves from their chains, even when they are broken and have fallen about their ankles. This is usually because despite being sorry for their sin and having confessed and heartily repented, they just cannot bring themselves to believe that God has forgiven them. Somehow they seem unable to realize that Christ really has paid the price for their sin and they are acquitted. So instead of stepping clear and going forth to serve the Lord in newness of life, they shuffle around with the chains still round their feet, which renders them just as ineffective as they were when bound.

If you are having trouble with your chains, do ask someone to help you. In fact, in this whole matter of confession and repentance it is not a bad idea to go occasionally to a minister or some other wise and experienced counsellor whom you trust, especially at those times when you are aware of a long established sin such as I have been writing about. He or she will be able to help you get things in perspective, to see clearly what is sin and what is not, and help you to realize the glorious truth that you really are free. 'Ransomed, healed, restored, forgiven.' Accept God's forgiveness and the freedom Christ has won for you. You are free to begin to 'go forth in holiness'.

There remains the problem of actual bondage. I used to wonder very much how it was possible for a believer to be in bondage, but I have learnt from people who are experienced in the ministry of deliverance that it is indeed possible, and it seems fairly clear that this may come about for any of the following reasons:

(a) Failure on the part of the believer to thoroughly renounce sin. In chapter 1 I touched on this briefly, and I used the term 'harbouring the enemy'. I think that is a good way of putting it. By persisting in known sin a person allows the enemy first to gain a foothold in their life, and then opens wide the door and lets him right in. If he is allowed to stay he will settle down and make himself really at home, and it will be much harder to get him out later on.

This is also true of deliberate disobedience to God and failure on our part to yield the whole of our lives to Christ. Remember the illustration I used in chapter 1 of the war having been won, but there still being some pockets of enemy resistance. This is true in our own personal lives also. Christ has done his part, but we are responsible for handing over to him the whole of our territory. If we allow Satan even the tiniest corner we are not free, and be assured he will seek, and probably find opportunities for extending his area of control.

(b) There are some things which, if engaged in, very quickly and effectively open the door to Satan; such things as sexual perversion, pornography, alcoholism and the use of hard drugs, and failure to exercise control over one's temper, especially when this leads to violence.

These things may have been engaged in before conversion, or before a believer came to a full understanding of what he or she was doing – perhaps while quite young. If at some point in a believer's life anything like this from the past has been renounced and dealt with, then there will be no problem, but if they have just been buried and not dealt with it is vital to deal with them now.

(c) I suppose I need hardly say to Christians that engagement in occult activities of any kind – spiritualism, witchcraft, fetishes, fortune-telling, yoga, astrology, and many other things – is deliberate disobedience to God and a personal invitation to Satan. If there is, or ever has been, any involvement of this kind in your life, it must be confessed and renounced if this has not already been done. Paul treats such things very seriously indeed, urging us to put them out of our lives (Col 3:5, 8), and he warns us that people who indulge in them will not inherit the kingdom of God (Gal 5:19-21; 1 Cor 6:9-10).

For a believer it is usually sufficient to confess these things and make a hearty and true repentance and renunciation. This, together with the sure knowledge of God's redeeming and forgiving love, will restore the Christian to a full relationship with him. The enemy will have no option but to relinquish the territory he once held, and this will be filled instead by the Holy Spirit. Remember to ask him to come and fill you, and go on being filled by him.

It may be, however, that Satan has been able to establish such a hold upon a person, even a believer (though I
think this is rare), that deliverance ministry is necessary.
It is unwise and may even be dangerous to enter into this
kind of activity without knowing what you are doing, so
if you realize that this is what is needed, then seek the
help of someone wise and experienced in this ministry,
and do not delay. Satan must be told to go.

It is possible for someone, even a Christian, to be in
bondage because of the occult activity of someone else,
usually someone close to them, and it may well be something in the past of which the affected person is hardly or
not at all aware. Perhaps I can best illustrate this from
my own experience.

When I was seven years old my father died, and my
mother gave birth to her third child who died within a
few months. In her sorrow my mother turned for comfort
and help to the only friends who were near at the time,
and these 'friends' led her into spiritualism. Her involvement with spiritualism did not last long – she was a
Christian and remained so all her life – but during this
brief, unhappy period she took my two little brothers
and me to be 'named' at the spiritualist church – though I
had, in fact, been baptized. For years the name given to
me by the spiritualists was tagged on to my Christian
names. Then, realizing in my teens that it had not been
given to me at baptism, I stopped using it.

The sequel to all this came many years later when, as
an adult, Spirit-filled Christian, I was aware of a block in
my life. Many times I asked the Lord what it was that
seemed to prevent me from being utterly his in the way I
so much desired. It was as though I could go so far with
the Lord and then I came up against a wall so real I could
almost feel it. Eventually during a residential conference,
the ministry and teaching made me so acutely aware of
this barrier that I really cried to the Lord. Standing in a

hall full of women praising God, my spirit cried out, 'What is it, Lord?' and straightaway into my mind came the words, 'It's faith. You haven't enough faith,' which surprised me a lot, as I thought I *had* faith. However, I accepted this as coming from the Lord, and with all the singing going on around me I just spoke out loud that one word 'faith'.

Then the Lord did a beautiful thing. During the ministry which followed the time of praise, a lovely servant of his was speaking to us, and at one point he held up his hand, looked straight in my direction and said, 'Receive the anointing of faith!' and I knew God had done everything that was necessary. Those words were of special significance to a number of women at that conference, but the speaker knew nothing of their particular relevance to me, until I went to him afterwards and shared what had happened. He prayed with me for a confirmation of what God had done, and as he laid hands upon me and began to pray, the Holy Spirit came upon me and I found myself on the floor, 'resting in him'. While I rested there he called to mind that 'naming' ceremony from so long ago, which I had not even thought of for many years. That was where my blockage came from, for the name I had been given in the spiritualist church was Faith. How mighty and wonderful and gracious is the Lord! I had been bound in that one particular area of faith. Now I was *free*. The wall was no more.

I am happy to say that my mother also was fully released from the effects of her own involvement with spiritualism, just before she died at eighty-five years old, beautifully, peacefully – and free.

Now don't go ferreting around trying to nose out something that may not even be there, but if you are seeking the Lord and opening your heart to him you will be aware of it if there is something coming between you. If you really don't know what it is, ask him, and seek the help of a wise counsellor. If you love God and want to be utterly his, tell him so and ask him to reveal and take away anything which is preventing the union with him which you so desire. He will do it.

There is more to holiness than not sinning and not being in bondage, though these things have to be dealt with before we can really start. Just as sin has more to do with our sinful *attitude* than with the individual sins which we commit, so it is not so much what we *do* that makes us holy, but what we *are*. We are called to be whole, to be completely what God intends us to be. As human beings we share certain common attributes and we must allow the Holy Spirit to strengthen and develop those attributes, along with all the characteristics and personality traits which are uniquely ours, so that we become that 'undivided, unbroken, individual entity' of which I wrote earlier, and are able to function 'duly, easily and satisfactorily' in that state of life to which it has pleased God to call us. This is holiness.

If God has called you to be a wife and mother, then he will want to develop your sexuality and your maternal instincts to the full, in the way that is suited to that vocation. And to your wifehood and your motherhood you will also bring those special gifts of humour, wisdom, insight, patience, forbearance, tenderness, or whatever, which go to make up your own unique personality.

If on the other hand you are called to live the single life, those characteristics and attributes which are common to women will be there just the same, but they will be developed and directed to suit *your* calling, and again all your own special qualities will be added too.

The secret is to get to know yourself and to give the Holy Spirit absolute freedom with every part of you. Anyone who has had experience of working with prisoners would agree that what happens to the prisoner when he or she comes out of prison is of supreme importance and usually plays a great part in determining whether that person 'goes straight' in future, or ends up back in prison.

For the Christian, stepping free from the tangle of chains, there is also the possibility of returning to captivity. We know about the demon who goes off and finds all his friends, inviting them to come back and occupy the clean and tidy house, and we know what to do to prevent this happening. But having let the Holy Spirit in, we must allow him to really occupy the premises. The decorating and the furnishing must be of his choosing, though we may have to wield the paint brush.

Someone I know was set free a short while ago from a burden she had borne for a long time, and from the guilt, fear and inhibitions which had accompanied this burden. In this new state of freedom she went around for quite a while plaintively enquiring of the Lord, herself and her friends, 'But who *am* I?' This is not as strange as it sounds. In her case her uncertainty about herself was highlighted by her particular circumstances, but we all need to know ourselves, and to recognize which gifts from God make us ourselves. To follow the example of another well-known song, each one of us should be able to thank our Father 'for making me me'.

So far I have not mentioned the physical healing which often occurs spontaneously when people are set free. Many people will testify to the reality of this, and it is a cause for rejoicing and thankfulness, but what of those who have some permanent physical disability or illness – those who are not healed? Does this prevent them from being that 'unbroken, individual entity', that 'complete system'? Does it mean that they cannot hope to function 'duly, easily and satisfactorily'? By ordinary definition, to be physically handicapped or disabled in some way does mean that this is not altogether possible, but it would be absurd to suggest that holiness is not for such people. I have deliberately used the phrase 'in that state of life to which it has pleased God to call us' in connection with 'wholeness', and to that I would add, 'or in whatever circumstances we find ourselves'. Surely the evidence is that as the Holy Spirit is permitted to have complete control over every part of a person's being, even the damaged body is taken by him and moulded into the 'complete system' which is the truly holy person.

I make bold enough to suggest that accepting and coming to terms with disability is, for those who have to do it, part of the process of 'knowing ourselves', which is essential for all of us. I speak humbly here, very conscious of the fact that I have no personal experience or testimony to offer, and full of admiration for those gallant people whose holy lives bear eloquent testimony to the truth of what I have written. There are plenty of them about.

For all of us, whatever our individual circumstances, there is no need to be desperately introspective about this business of knowing ourselves. What matters most is our attitude towards God, that infinite desire of the heart of which St Teresa wrote. If we have that, we shall be constantly looking at him, and less and less at ourselves, and he will do in us what we could never accomplish on our own.

Even a flawless diamond, when it has been cut and shaped and polished many times, is beautiful only because of the way it reflects the light. We shall be holy only to the extent that we reflect the holiness of God, when we allow him to shape us and polish us, and when we stand constantly in the light of his glory.

> Make me like a precious stone,
> Crystal clear and finely honed.
> Life of Jesus shining through,
> Giving glory back to you.
>
> D. Bryant, © Thankyou Music 1978.

9

An Intercessor in the Family

The changes that begin to take place in us when we say yes to God often come as a surprise to us. They often surprise our families also! I remember Chris Leage, the English national leader of Lydia, telling of how a husband came up to her one day and said, 'I don't know what it is you are doing to my wife in Lydia, but whatever it is, I like it! Please keep doing it!' Of course, Lydia in itself wasn't doing anything to his wife. It was the Lord. In company with so many others, that woman was being changed as she responded to God, and the effect was being felt by her husband and her family. Because she had turned her face towards the Lord she was beginning to blossom into all the fullness of what it means to be a woman, as surely as the bud blossoms on the bough in springtime.

For anyone who says yes to God's call to be an intercessor, anyone who is prepared to open their heart to him and to the whole world, the experience is bound to be life-changing. Unfortunately, the response of those nearest and dearest is not always as enthusiastic (at first, anyway) as that of the husband who spoke to Chris. We need to remember that what is happening to us, both in our intercession groups and within ourselves, is *our* experience, and not necessarily theirs, so unless we are

105

sensitive and able to share lovingly with our families, and perhaps especially our husbands, they may well be puzzled and even suspicious of what we are doing and the effect it is having upon us.

It is important that we understand where we fit into the framework of the family, and that our husbands understand this also. If we are women and married, then whatever new work God may ask us to do we remain first and foremost wives, and meeting the firm commitment of praying as part of a group requires the co-operation of our husbands. For the single woman the considerations are different, but nonetheless real, and she will have her own family and others about her who will be affected by the changes in herself and perhaps in her pattern of life.

For many women the experience of being intercessors has brought a new confidence as each one has learnt to share herself in a new way within the group, and especially as she has become more aware of her position and authority as a child of God in her own right. Where one person in a family is called to something different, or seems to be moving forward alone in a new way in the Christian life, there can be difficulties. Where there is maturity and sensitivity there will be no problem; the one will recognize the call and the ministry of the other, and be supportive and encouraging. Where the partners in marriage have their relationship firmly rooted in Christ, and where the wife is truly and securely under the loving headship of her husband who really loves her as his own flesh (see Eph 5:21-33), there is nothing to fear. However, no matter how committed and loving a couple may be, such a relationship does not usually come into being as soon as they have said, 'I do.' It takes practice, and somewhere along the line this matter of learning to accept and encourage a wife's (or a husband's) ministry may be part of growing into that perfect partnership.

I give thanks for the many husbands who lovingly and generously encourage their wives and give them the freedom to do what God is asking of them, even when they themselves are not quite sure what this intercession business is all about. A lack of knowledge or understanding about intercession can be one of the chief causes of dissension. A husband may be suspicious, or just doubtful about the validity of this ministry simply because it is outside his own experience, and he may feel unwilling, or unable, to set his wife free. He may be alarmed at the growing confidence and assurance he observes in her, seeing it as a threat to their relationship and the status quo, rather than recognizing it as something which could transform their lives most beautifully. Or the poor man may simply be dumbfounded when his erstwhile argumentative and strong-willed wife begins to display unusual gentleness and even submissiveness! It is not to be wondered at if, having spent a number of years relating to her as she was, he has difficulty at first in adjusting to the new woman who now inhabits his home and shares his bed.

Talking of sharing his bed, I know of at least one husband who is still somewhat bemused at the change that came over his love life when his wife began to be a 'whole' woman, so that her sexuality, too, was set free to be the holy thing God intended it should be. 'Male and female created he them.' Perhaps you are beginning to see why I speak of being surprised at what God does in us when we say yes! And if what you have just read surprises you, ask yourself these questions: Do you ever remember to thank God for your sexuality? For your love life? To praise him for the delight he gives you in each other? If the answer is no, could it be that along the way to wholeness and holiness God is waiting to change this part of your life? Many marriages have been transformed in this way, and this is often the key which unlocks the doors to holiness and freedom in other parts of our life also, and ultimately even in what we are pleased to call our ministries. Just another of the Holy Spirit's delightful surprises.

For some women the call to intercession may also be a call to leadership, and although this may only mean leadership of a small group it can be a new and unfamiliar thing for some. If the church background is one in which women are not expected or encouraged to lead anything, this may cause problems with husbands or pastors. However, when God calls us he gives us the anointing of his lovely Holy Spirit, and where this is present his grace and enabling will be there to smooth the way if we are only loving, patient and sensitive.

The Christian life is full of paradoxes, and this is another, that it is only the woman who is confident and sure of herself in the sight of God who is able to be truly gentle and submissive. She alone can enter into the kind of relationship where she is able to be a full and equal partner in the marriage while at the same time acknowledging and rejoicing in the proper authority and protection of her husband (Eph 5:21-33; 1 Pet 3:1-6). It may be as a result of the new experience of 'wholeness' that for the first time a couple begin to seriously consider what their marriage should be in the sight of God. The changes in his wife, however welcome, may force a man to rethink his position as head of the family, and if he has not yet become free himself he may well feel challenged, or even threatened, especially if he has never been the head of the family in any real sense. Such a situation calls for patience and lots of tender, loving care on the part of the wife. She may even have to wait for a while before being able to become part of a praying group. She need have no fear, however. If God is calling her to this ministry he will make her path straight in his own way and in his time. The changes in her will speak for themselves and her husband may be won 'without a word' (1 Pet 3:1).

It is interesting to note that Peter finishes his exhort-ation to husbands and wives with the words 'in order that your prayers may not be hindered' (1 Pet 3:7). I think that little phrase speaks volumes, for our prayer *will* be hindered if this closest of all human relationships is not right, which is why I am devoting so much time and space to it. Does this mean that it is impossible to be an effective intercessor if all is not yet well in our marriage or family situation? No, I do not believe so, but it does mean that we have to make sure the channels are open, on our side at least, for God to do his healing and trans-forming work.

If you want to have an understanding of a major part of Satan's strategy in these times, take a good, hard look at some of the obvious evils of the age and see where their impact is felt most. The family is the natural, God-given unit of society, and Satan understands very well that the strength and well-being of a nation depends to a great extent upon the security and stability of its family life. He has, therefore, a vested interest in undermining and, if possible destroying normal, healthy family life in any way he can. The Christian family is not spared his attentions. It would be unhealthy and quite wrong for us to be always obsessively looking out for 'satanic attacks' upon our family life, because most of the problems that arise are due to our own shortcomings or to the ordinary adjustments people have to make all the time when they live closely together. However, it would equally be a mistake to disregard altogether the possibility of enemy activity. After all, the intercessor has enlisted in an army engaged in spiritual warfare, bent upon reclaiming ter-ritory from Satan, and he is hardly likely to take that lying down. However strong we may be on our own be-half, most of us are very vulnerable when anything touches our nearest and dearest, or our relationship with them. Satan will exploit this to the full, given half a chance, and sometimes he doesn't have to try very hard. Our own enthusiasm and lack of sensitivity will do most of his work for him. If he can sow the seeds of misunderstanding and dissension between members of a family, and especially between husband and wife, he will feel himself well on the way to putting at least one prayer warrior out of action.

Therefore, 'Be watchful. Your adversary the devil prowls around . . . seeking someone to devour. Resist him, firm in your faith' (1 Pet 5:8-9). You know your authority as a child of God. Whenever you spot the danger signals rebuke Satan, send him from you, and take that problem – whatever it is – quickly to the Lord (Jas 4:7-8). If you can do this together, so much the better.

So far I have been writing in general terms about the kind of problems which may arise in ordinary families, but some women called into intercession are having to cope with very serious situations, even tragedy. Some may be married to unbelievers, but even Christian men can sometimes succumb to what I have called the evils of the age.

Only the woman who has an alcoholic husband can tell you of the fear and agony involved as she watches him kill himself. Though he may not actually die for a long time, she will watch the inevitable deterioration of his health and his faculties, the coarseness which overtakes what may once have been a sensitive and attractive personality, and the spiritual blindness which follows as surely as night follows day. Bitter and many are the tears she will shed.

Only the woman whose husband delights in pornographic literature and films can explain to you how cheap this makes her feel, how diminished, and how it can rob their personal life of its romance and joy.

Only she who has been beaten can tell you of the degradation and loss of human dignity, as well as of the pain and injury. The agony of verbal onslaught can be every bit as devastating as physical attack, especially when it takes the form of accusation and condemnation.

Only the woman whose husband has been unfaithful and who has lived through it knows the searing of the tearing asunder of what God has joined into one flesh.

There can be no joyful resting in the headship of their husbands for such women.

I could go on to mention the compulsive gambler, the petty thief, the habitual criminal. The list would be long. These things do not afflict all of us, nor do they necessarily last a lifetime, but I have met enough women intercessors struggling with these kind of problems to cause me to ponder deeply the mystery of the suffering of God's servants. How many women have cried out, 'Why, Lord? Why, when I love you and him so much, when I have prayed to you and cared for him, when I long for nothing more than for us both to be totally yours, together, should these things be?' I wish I could say I had all the answers. I haven't, though I believe I have begun to know some of them.

Of course you may say there are always two sides to every question. What caused a man to be what he is in the first place? Does the wife have anything to answer for in these situations? I have placed this chapter in the wake of the previous two quite deliberately, for I am assuming that the women to whom I address these words are those who have at least begun to travel the road to humility, wholeness and holiness which I have already outlined; that they have either repented, or are now willing to repent, of their own mistakes and allow the Holy Spirit to do his work in them.

How can these women come to the foot of the cross and lay down their heavy burdens, and open their hearts freely to the sufferings of the world as intercessors? Is it possible? I tell you it is, and they do.

The first essential thing for an intercessor, and indeed for any woman in such circumstances, is that she be in the right position in relation to her husband and the Lord. The right relation to your husband is loving, humble submission. Oh, yes it is! Loving submission in the sense described by Paul and Peter, which does *not* mean miserable subjection or servitude. Note Ephesians 5:21. We are all told to be in subjection to one another (see also Gal 5:13; Phil 2:3; 1 Pet 5:5). This applies to all within the church and the family, but it has a special application for husbands and wives because of their unique relationship and the special responsibility one has for the other.

If your husband is not fulfilling his proper role in the partnership it may not be possible for you to completely fulfil yours, and this will inevitably make unnatural demands upon you. You may have to make decisions, be strong, and sometimes act in a way that would not be necessary if *he* was in a right relationship with *you*, and with God, but once again it is attitude that makes all the difference. The readiness and willingness to fill the role of a wife in the proper, God-directed way.

Here is another mystery to ponder – the mystery of the 'one flesh'. Although you are a separate individual, in a real way you have become one with your husband. This relationship is so close that it has been described as 'signifying the mystical union that is betwixt Christ and his church' (*Book of Common Prayer*), and which Paul described as a 'profound mystery' (Eph 5:32). This means that his pains, his temptations, his fears and his failures are yours also. This does not mean that you are guilty of his sins, but it does mean that in a mysterious way, and more than is possible in any other relationship, you are involved with everything he does or that affects him; you suffer when he suffers.

This sounds like an impossible burden to bear, but, paradoxically again, to accept this is to be set free to serve God in a special way. It is the principle of death and resurrection. By dying to self for your husband you will be raised to glorious freedom in God's service. 'Precious in the sight of the Lord is the death of his saints' (Ps 116:15).

Has it ever occurred to you how privileged you are to have one of God's sick and needy children in your own home to minister to? Have you ever thought how much God must love *you* and esteem *you* to trust you with this man who is so needy? God must trust you to be steadfast in your love towards himself, and in your obedience and patience. He must believe that you are capable of this and he must trust you to be steadfast also in your love for your husband. How else could he entrust this wounded, sick child of his into your hands? For your part, you must trust him. Maintain constantly your own attitude of purity and holiness, but do not judge or condemn your husband. Instead, love him and serve him, tend him and cherish him, and 'if there is any excellence, if there is anything worthy of praise, think about these things' (Phil 4:8).

Your right position in relation to God is that of a daughter of the King! Humble before him, yes, but realizing your own worth in his sight. I want to emphasize this, because so many women who are abused in one way or another by their husbands, or even just taken for granted and 'put upon' by the rest of the family or friends, lose their dignity and self-respect. Yet God esteems you worthy and precious and beautiful. So look up, you are a princess! Put on your 'holy array' (1 Pet 3:4) and praise your King, whose steadfast love for *you* endures for ever.

The relationship between husband and wife as father and mother is at the heart of a normal, healthy family life. Satan does not want children to grow up knowing God, so he attacks parents. It is through our relationship with our earthly fathers that we first begin to have some inkling of a relationship with God as our heavenly Father, his wisdom and righteousness, his provision for us, and perhaps through our mothers we learn something of his tenderness and loving mercy. God has provided in his wisdom for children to be nurtured and brought up to know and love him under the guidance and protection of their earthly parents, whose care for them is complementary. The evils of which I wrote in chapter 1 strike right at the heart of the family, spoiling the relationship between parents and children, and between children and those they meet outside their homes, for it is within the healthy family circle that relationships and attitudes are worked out and children made ready and able to take their places in the world at large. Is it any wonder, then, that so many young people have no knowledge of God and neither love nor fear him? But however much we love and nurture our children we cannot keep them from contact with other people whose standards are very different from our own, in a world which can be confusing at the least, and at worst dangerous and frightening. The agony of parents whose children have gone astray cannot be described. Oh, the cries of anguish which the Lord hears! And he *does* hear, be assured of that. Never underestimate the keeping power of God, and his power to keep them wherever they are and whatever they may be doing, and to bring them back into the shelter of his arms.

I would like to suggest that there is a very special role here for grandmothers (and grandfathers, too, I daresay), as intercessors within the family. Grandmothers can survey the scene from the vantage point of their own experience of bringing up a family – experience they wish they'd had before they started! As they look back they may find that they have learnt not only how to love, teach, train, control and release their children, but how to pray for them.

Make good use of that experience now as you intercede for your children and your children's children. You probably have more time now than when your family was growing up, and with your special knowledge of them you are in a unique position to bring them before the Lord and wait upon him on their behalf, seeking the inspiration of the Holy Spirit and offering the prayer of faith with confidence and authority.

The unofficial 'aunts' of this world have a very special place too. I think of one lovely daughter of the King as I write this. The feet of many young people – and their parents – beat a path to her door in search of unbiased, objective sympathy and counsel, which they receive in full measure, but more even than this, she holds them before the Lord in prayer. Truly, she has many children and there are many like her.

I have not yet mentioned such things as the untimely death of a young child, or long-term illness or disability of one's self or one's loved ones. Suffering comes in many ways and few people, if any, escape it altogether, but I cannot help noticing that many people, especially women, who are called by God to be intercessors are those who have lived through, or are now living through, times of great trial and sorrow.

There's an old saying, 'If you have a child in need of loving care, give it to the woman who already has half a dozen.' Perhaps a similar principle applies to intercessors, in that the heart of love which has borne grief with humility and patience – the humble heart again – and has learnt to gaze steadfastly still into the face of the Father, is a heart able to take unto itself the grief of the whole world and share his love and his compassion in a very special way. The principle of death and resurrection. Dying to self through accepted suffering and in loving service, raised with joy to the privilege of co-operating with God as his intercessors.

10

The Way of Loneliness

The way of an intercessor is the way of loneliness, for some of us all the time, and for all of us some of the time.

When we think of loneliness, perhaps we think in terms of an old lady living by herself, who can't go out, and nobody comes to see her. That is one kind of loneliness, but loneliness, like suffering, wears many different disguises.

We are the body of Christ. Together we worship him. Together we serve him. Together we continue his complete work here on earth. Yet at the same time we stand before him as our individual selves and his call comes to each one of us *alone*. Look at the stories of Noah, Abraham and Samuel. See how alone they were when God spoke to them. And how lonely they were in their response! It was Noah alone who heard the word of the Lord concerning his great grief over the world that he had made. To Abraham alone came the call and the responsibility for leading his family out of their homeland to go they knew not where. Samuel, alone in the night, heard the word of the Lord. Andrew and Simon, James and John and Philip, each heard Jesus speak his name and call him to himself individually. Jesus did not say, 'Andrew,' (or James or Philip), 'I want you to go out and gather together a band of likely young men to be

117

my disciples.' He called them as individuals. And he stands now and speaks my name, and yours, saying, 'Follow me.' Where will we follow him? And how far are we prepared to go? Christ puts these questions to us and each one of us has to answer them *alone*. It has to be so, for whatever our situation we cannot be certain of travelling companions.

Lydia Prince (whose story is told in *Appointment in Jerusalem,* Kingsway Publications) gave up her good job, disposed of her possessions, turned her back on the man who wanted to marry her, and went off to Jerusalem – alone – and only God knew why. Jackie Pullinger (*Chasing the Dragon,* Hodder & Stoughton) took herself off to Hong Kong – alone – and only God knew why. Noah built the ark, Abraham packed up and left home, and only God knew why. Not many of us are called to that particular kind of service, but make no mistake about it, the response and the commitment Christ calls for from each one of us is the same. His commitment to us is absolute; should ours to him be anything less? We sing so easily in our hymns of this love, so amazing and so divine, that it demands everything from us in return. Dare we give this much?

Paul said, 'Whatever gain I had, I counted as loss for the sake of Christ. Indeed I count everything as loss because of the surpassing worth of knowing Christ Jesus my Lord. For his sake I have suffered the loss of all things, and count them as refuse, in order that I may gain Christ' (Phil 3:7-8).

It is when we are truly able to say these words that the way begins to get lonely, for few are prepared to go that far, and the further you go the lonelier it may turn out to be. What? Even within the church, the body of Christ? Yes, even there. When we come to die no one will be able to go with us, and in this dying to self, here on earth, in order that we may 'gain Christ and be found in him', we must go it alone. Others may point us in the right direction, set us on the path, and greet us on the way, but we alone can put our feet into his footsteps and follow him.

What does this mean for us as intercessors? For a great many of us, the call to be an intercessor, heard and answered individually, will lead us into fellowship with others who have heard the same call. We shall become part of a praying group, and the group may be part of a larger fellowship. The bond of love and fellowship between people united by God in this way is beautiful and precious. However, it was in the midst of a wonderful gathering of his intercessors, surrounded by the love and companionship and encouragement of my sisters in the Lydia Fellowship, that I heard God saying to me, 'Audrey, what if it wasn't like this? What if there was no singing, no rejoicing, no sharing and no encouragement? What if you were quite alone? Would you still be prepared to follow where I lead?' I cried to the Lord that night, I can tell you, and like Abraham I fell on my face before him. I had to kick out all the props from under me and lean on him alone. To be really alone with God is awesome, but he wants to hear from us that we are willing for this. Willing to have him and him alone. Yes, of course, he gives us each other, but if he is to totally direct our lives and share with each one of us the burden of his heart, then there are times when we must stand before him quite alone, stripped of every prop and consolation. It can be a very lonely place. When people so glibly say, 'Oh well, no matter what happens you are never really alone,' of course they are right, but I can't help wondering whether they have ever been really alone with God. We are so conditioned to relying upon one another.

Jesus was often alone.

'After he had dismissed the crowds, he went up into

the hills by himself to pray. When evening came, he was there alone' (Mt 14:23).

'And in the morning, a great while before day, he rose and went out to a lonely place, and there he prayed' (Mk 1:35).

'He said to his disciples, "Sit here, while I go yonder and pray." . . . and he came to the disciples and found them sleeping' (Mt 26:36, 40).

Alone he went into the wilderness to face the temptations of the devil (Mk 1:12-13), and who can plumb the mystery of that terrible cry from the cross, 'My God, my God, why hast thou forsaken me?'?

The true intercessor will always be called to walk in the way of loneliness for some of the time, and some will be called to walk that way all of the time.

We may not be called to leave our homes and go away to live in isolation or in a strange place, to be separated from our fellows in that sense, but we are being called to be 'separated' in a way, for we are called to be 'set apart' for God, for the work he has given us to do, and this will sometimes separate us from those around us.

Other people have certain expectations of us, and when we do not meet those expectations they find it disconcerting. How they react depends upon what sort of people they are. Even the most loving and accepting family may ask, 'Why? Why so many hours in prayer? Why so many days in fasting?'

The call to intercession is costly in time and commitment, and the cost may well be paid in terms of the understanding or approval of other people. We are in a tricky situation here, for if we try to explain to everyone what our commitment is, what it is that we are doing, some will understand it, but to others it will be a challenge or a threat if they themselves are as yet unwilling to tread uncompromisingly the path God is indicating for them, and our position seems to them to be that of 'holier than thou'. Sometimes misunderstanding arises simply because not everyone has quite grasped the reality of the body of Christ, with every member having his or her own individual part to play, and the total work of Christ in the church being dependent upon everyone doing their own thing as directed by him. Sadly, such people often have their eyes so fixed on what God has given them to do that they cannot appreciate the importance, or even the validity, of what he has given someone else to do. It is a painful thing that this should cause misunderstanding or even division, but it does, and intercession can often seem to be the poor relation among ministries, simply because it is invisible. It is easier to see most other things being done in the church, while prayer can become what you do when you've done everything else!

In these days of renewal in the church and of greater sharing of work and ministry among all the people, many clergy wives are experiencing greater freedom to be what God wants them to be as individuals. However, in days gone by, and in some places still, the expectations of people concerning the wives of their ministers amounted in some cases to burdens grievous to be borne. To tread the path indicated by God rather than that expected by other people, for such women, could be a lonely walk indeed, fraught at least with misunderstanding and probably with condemnation too. As well as being a wife to my husband, mother to the family, and coping with all those unpredictable happenings peculiar to the vicarage, God has given me two things to do for him: to be an intercessor – and for some years this also meant being in leadership – and, more recently, to write. Both require a great deal of time and commitment; both are 'invisible', at least while I am doing them. From my husband I receive a full measure of loving support and encouragement for both, which has sometimes been quite costly for him too. People know and understand what I do, but this is not the case for everybody. One lady in a similar situation to mine has been made very aware of the people who look askance because she does not play a greater part in organizing the 'activities' of the parish. She hasn't quite been what *they* expect a clergy wife to be. 'I don't mind them not understanding,' she said. 'It's their condemnation that hurts.' That's a kind of loneliness.

Being misunderstood is not peculiar to clergy wives, though they may be particularly vulnerable in some ways and in some places, but anyone who sets out to follow a course not understood or appreciated by the rest of her church or fellowship must be prepared to walk in loneliness even in the midst of the joy and exuberance of a renewed congregation. That can be one of the loneliest places on earth. It is a sadness, in these days, that many Christians find *all* their joy and companionship in gathering together in praise and worship (good though that is) and have lost the habit of coming apart for a while. They seem to have lost the desire for a closer fellowship with God alone, and therefore do not understand the lonely walk which an ever deepening commitment to him may sometimes lead us to.

Many people have 'aloneness' thrust upon them, and not just those who actually live alone. Even for those of us who are called into groups and fellowships of intercessors, there are still times when God calls us to wait on him by ourselves – alone with him, perhaps, in the night watches – but for some this aloneness in prayer is all the time. The wife whose husband cannot, or will not release her, will not only be denied the fellowship and support of others, but will know the loneliness of not being able to share what she does with the one who is nearest to her, or having his approval and support. Her way as an intercessor will be lonely, but if he is a Christian there will at least be the hope that one day he will hear God speak concerning this matter and will respond. For the woman married to an unbeliever the way is harder still, because *all* her response to God, in every part of her life, must be made in the most profound loneliness, that of being 'separated' in this from the person dearest to her, the man with whom she is one flesh.

I know one beautiful Christian lady who is in just that situation, and I admire her more than I can say. She acknowledges her difficulties, but I have never once heard her complain about her husband; rather she praises his goodness to her and his kindness, and she loves God and does what she can. She is full of laughter, fun and sympathy. Her door is always open, and many people go to her to pour out their joys and their sorrows. She said to me one day, 'Audrey, I think I must have the biggest pair of ears in the parish!' I reckon she has, and a heart to match. I hope her 'loneliness' is softened in some measure by the love and appreciation which so many people have for her, and the extent to which she *is* able to share with other Christians.

That lady has found the answer. It is what I call passing through the acceptance barrier. I remember reading years ago that the first man to go through the sound barrier, albeit accidentally, was the pilot of a Hurricane fighter plane. Coming down (very rapidly!) in a steep dive, he found his controls quite useless, until he pushed the stick in the opposite direction to what was usual in those circumstances. Immediately the plane began to pull out of the dive. Now I do not know a thing about aeronautics, but I believe that conditions of flight are very different on the other side of the sound barrier. They certainly are on the other side of the acceptance barrier. Most of us fret and fume, or bewail our difficulties, or strive to overcome them (and sometimes, of course, we *should* be able to overcome them). Eventually we may even become resigned to them, but that is not the same thing as accepting them. To be able to say, as my lovely friend has done, 'Here I am, in this particular situation. For the moment, anyway, there is not a thing I can do about changing it, but God has put me here, or at least permitted me to be here, so what is he saying to me *here and now?* No matter what goes on around me, I can walk with him and do his perfect will *here.*' That is not to abandon hope. It is to pass through the acceptance barrier, and on the other side it is quite different, and much more peaceful. We come out of the dive. We start going up instead of down.

So it can be with all our areas of loneliness. I wish I understood more of what it means to live alone. I have never done that in my life. To live alone is not necessarily to be lonely, and indeed I know more than one person who is glad and thankful sometimes to get back into her own little nook and shut the door in blissful aloneness – a state which is not too easily come by if you live in a family.

One of my single friends has spoken to me of the temptation to become too independent, born initially of necessity perhaps, but gradually over the years growing into a protective shell around her, keeping other people out. Another has told me that this single independence became the pride of her life, until she recognized it for what it was and allowed God to deal with it. This kind of loneliness is not God-sent.

I can readily appreciate that living alone can offer special opportunities for an intercessor, but whether living alone or in families there are many people who are obliged to take the way of an intercessor by themselves. This may be for any of the reasons I have indicated, and probably many others, such as having a young family, but sometimes it is quite simply the way God has called them. Some people have a special responsibility to be

watchmen in their own community, church or fellowship. They may be people who are not able to play a very
physically active part in what goes on, but quietly and
unobtrusively they are watching and observing, allowing
the Holy Spirit to pinpoint for them the special needs
which he wants them to pray about. Sometimes they may
have full knowledge of what is needed; often they will
simply recognize that a certain person is 'in need', and
without knowing anything more they will lovingly hold
that person before the Lord, allowing the Holy Spirit to
'make intercession for them' (Rom 8:26-27).

For most of us, then, most of the time, we shall have
the precious companionship of our brothers and sisters
in Christ, be they intercessors or not, but sometimes
God will require us to travel with him alone. Some of
our brothers and sisters may find the going too rough.
Some of the disciples did. They found the things Jesus
put before them too much to accept and many of them
'drew back and no longer went about with him' (Jn
6:66).

For those who do continue along the lonely road there
comes the consolation of a deeper companionship with
God than would have been possible any other way. God
has a special care for those who are called the fatherless
and widows, and this, I believe, we can take also to mean
all those who are desolate and 'lonely', like the wife of
an alcoholic who said one day, 'I know what it is to be
bereaved though my husband is still alive.' Like those
who are 'separated', misunderstood and condemned.

'Father of the fatherless and protector of widows is
God in his holy habitation. God gives the desolate a
home to dwell in' (Ps 68:5-6).

When some of the disciples drew back, 'Jesus said to
the twelve, "Will you also go away?"

Simon Peter answered him, "Lord, to whom shall we
go? You have the words of eternal life"' (Jn 6:67-68).

For to this you have been called, because Christ also suffered for you, leaving you an example, that you should follow in his steps (1 Pet 2:21).

I I

Under Attack

. . . that you may be able to stand against the wiles of the devil (Eph 6:11).

At the moment when the Prime Minister announced that Britain had entered the Second World War, I was eating breakfast with my mother and brothers and sisters. We children were all agog with anticipation and full of questions. 'What would it mean to be at war? What would happen?'

Within a few minutes something did happen. The air raid sirens began to wail. My mother snatched up our peacefully sleeping cats and shut them in the kitchen, and then she shepherded the five of us children and the dog out towards our already sandbagged garage, which was to serve as a shelter. Halfway across the garden the dog slipped from her collar and bolted down the road with her tail between her legs, wailing like a banshee. At that point panic set in, and I began to shake with fear. We sat in the garage-shelter, clutching our newly issued gas masks, while all the grown-ups joined in little clusters by the gates, peering into the sky. Nothing was to be seen but a few barrage balloons riding gently on the breeze. I didn't cry, or scream, or indeed do anything, but I shook from head to toe with terror at what nameless horror might be about to fall on us from the sky.

Nothing did fall, and soon the all clear was sounded, the dog came home, and we all trooped indoors to finish our breakfast.

Eight months later, in the seaside town of Dover, we had been enjoying a beautiful spring. One night I had fallen asleep peacefully, in my room overlooking the sea, when suddenly all hell seemed to have been let loose. There were bangs and crashes and whistling noises and an ominous hiss – almost like rain falling, but what rain! We had had one thunder storm a few nights earlier, but I thought this must be the storm to end all storms. Then my mother came in. One look at her face and I knew this was no thunder storm, it was enemy attack. I was experiencing my first proper air raid.

A few months later still, in another town on the outskirts of London, my sister and I were taking the dog for a walk in that hour of an autumn evening just before the light begins to fade. The sky was a little overcast and as we walked we became aware of the gentle hum of an aircraft approaching us. It seemed to be very low, but there had been no warning sounded, so we paid little heed to it. Then suddenly, there it was coming across the roof-tops towards us – an enemy plane! It was very low indeed, so low that we could quite clearly see the men inside it looking down. That plane seemed to hang in the air in front of us, while we stood transfixed, gazing straight into the face of a German gunner. Then it was gone, but we didn't move for what seemed like ages, and I don't think we said a word till we got back home.

How could it happen? How could that plane have sneaked in, past all our defences, and just *be* there like that?

These little stories serve to illustrate three ways in which we may be affected by the enemy or come under his attack: the false alarm; the sudden violent outburst; and the crafty, sneaking-up tactic.

I have already written something about the operations of Satan, of how he has infiltrated our society and taken control of some parts of it; of how he will, if he is allowed to, attack and undermine our family life; and of how we are called to respond as intercessors, but in this chapter I want to take a personal look at the question of Satan's attacks upon us as individuals, and particularly in the context of our call to intercession.

First of all, we should never be on the defensive. There is no need for us to be. The victory has been won once and for all by Jesus Christ. If ever you find yourself fighting a rearguard action against Satan then something in your life must have gone very wrong indeed. 'The reason the Son of God appeared was to destroy the works of the devil' (1 Jn 3:8). He has done it! By his death he has destroyed him who has the power of death, that is, the devil (Heb 2:14). Christ reigns, and at the end he will deliver the kingdom to 'God the Father after destroying every rule and every authority and power' (1 Cor 15:24). Satan knows this well, and we must never forget it either. We fight from a position of victory, but like the defeated foe he is, knowing his time is running out, Satan is the one fighting a rearguard action, making attacks upon God's children where he can. Because we as intercessors are specifically engaged in spiritual warfare, committed to going right into what he still regards as his territory and reclaiming it, we are bound to attract his attentions in a personal way from time to time. How can we recognize his attacks, and how may we deal with them?

Like the Girl Guides and the Boy Scouts, our motto should be simply 'Be Prepared' and the first thing is to be aware of the ways in which the enemy may try to disturb you.

The first of my illustrations concerned the false alarm, and I place it first deliberately. We cannot attribute everything that goes wrong to enemy activity, and it is disconcerting to discover how many people try to do just that. At the first sign of something not being right the cry goes up, 'Help. Take cover. We're under attack!'

Satan must go laughing all the way to the gates of hell at the sight of Christians getting themselves all worked up on account of an attack that never was. While we are busy rebuking him our problem remains unsolved, for we haven't spotted the real cause which is probably our own sin. Our agitation and confusion will increase as long as we blame Satan instead of turning our attention to ourselves, and he won't have lifted a finger, except perhaps to stir things up a little.

Don't do his work for him.

It may simply be that we are persisting in something which we know to be wrong. Not wrong in itself maybe, but not in the will of God for us at that particular time. We have taken the decisions concerning the direction of our life into our own hands when they should be in the hands of God. 'Do not rely on your own insight . . . Be not wise in your own eyes' (Prov 3:5, 7).

It may be simply physical weakness. Have we gone on working too long and too late and allowed our judgement to be impaired by tiredness? Are we trying desperately to do something in our own strength, instead of allowing the Holy Spirit to fill us and enable us?

'In all your ways acknowledge him, and he will make straight your paths' (Prov 3:6). Allow the Holy Spirit to show you what is wrong and then allow him to deal with it quickly. Remember the prowling lion, on the watch for someone to devour. If we go round in circles trying to beat off attacks that haven't happened we shall soon become so confused that all he will have to do is to sit there and wait for us to fall into his jaws.

Sometimes, however, the attacks are all too real and Satan is not disposed to warn us that they are imminent.

The sudden, blistering assaults of the devil can be really frightening, but I sometimes think they are the easiest to deal with. The spiritual adrenalin flows, and we leap into victorious action. Sometimes, but not always.

A Christian couple had been through a particularly difficult time in their marriage. They had almost come to the point of separation, but eventually, after a great deal of honest and painful discussion and much prayer and forgiveness on both sides, they had been fully reconciled. They began to grow closer than ever before and this happy state of affairs continued for many months. One day they were sitting quietly, having a perfectly normal conversation, when suddenly, just like the air raid in my second story, all hell seemed to have been let loose. Recriminations and accusations were flying about all over the place and their new confidence and loving relationship, so patiently built up, came tumbling about their ears. The wife told me, 'I could hear what he was saying, and I could hear what I was saying, and I just couldn't believe those words were coming out of our mouths.'

Shattered and shaken afterwards, neither of them could really remember how it had all started. It was like having had an unexploded bomb in the house, with Satan seizing an opportunity to light the fuse. Eventually they both recognized that attack for what it was and Satan was sent packing, but it had been a sobering experience.

Sometimes a sudden attack may come in the form of an accident or illness. Again, we must be careful that we do not credit Satan with bringing about something which is really the result of our own folly or carelessness, or with making us ill when we have not been taking proper care of ourselves. We can hardly blame him if we drive our car at a reckless speed, or eat too much and make ourselves sick. Nevertheless, in his desperate attempts to put off the day of final reckoning, he does make physical assaults upon God's servants. I have already mentioned the sickness he would bring upon John Wesley in order to try and prevent him from preaching the gospel, but Wesley would press on in the power of the Spirit, and Satan would be obliged to leave him alone. The sickness would depart. Satan 'was a murderer from the beginning' (Jn 8:44); he tried on more than one occasion to kill Jesus before it was God's appointed time for him to die, and when any servant of God presents a real threat to him he will stop at nothing.

Sometimes, of course, God does allow the death of his servants, as in the case of Stephen and all the other martyrs past and present, and he also permits illness. But in every case where this is so, the circumstances may be used for his glory, his ultimate purposes will be served. Satan does not score.

When I stood with my sister on that autumn evening in 1940, gazing up at a German aeroplane, we were rooted to the spot and quite defenceless. I suppose if he had wanted to that pilot could have pressed a button and that would have been the end of two little girls and their dog. Where had he come from? How did he come to be there, when a moment before we had no idea that he was anywhere about?

I think I find these 'sneaking-up' tactics the most unnerving of all. In my own experience they often seem to occur just when I think I have everything nicely under control. Notice that I said when *I* have everything nicely under control! I have given everything to God, I am doing what I know he wants me to do, and perhaps I am engaged in some new project for him. All is going well. However, I haven't actually noticed Satan sitting at my elbow, whispering what a clever girl I am. But he's been there nevertheless, and presently I come to my senses – when things are *not* going so well – and I realize that slowly, imperceptibly, I have been taking things out of God's hands and into my own. I have been 'leaning unto my own understanding' – relying on my own insight (see Prov 3:5). Only the Lord knows how many times I have made a complete fool of myself in this way, or caused pain or embarrassment to someone else.

Sometimes, of course, the approach comes from a quite different angle, though it's just as subtle – especially if he can refer back to the kind of occasion I have just described. 'What makes you think you can do that? Remember what a disaster it was last time. You don't want to go through all that again, do you? Best not to get involved. Let someone else do it.'

For a writer a visit to a well-stocked Christian book-shop is enough to put them off writing for life if they listen to Satan. 'Look at all those books. Lots of them by really eminent Christians, too. Just look at the section on prayer! That one by Mr A. and another by Mr M. on intercession – a classic, that one. And what about the one by that lovely American lady? It's all been said before really, hasn't it? I should stick to writing letters if I were you!'

Whoever you are, whatever you do, he has the subtlest insinuations tailor-made for you.

Then there are the accusations. You will have noticed, of course, that when he accuses you he doesn't waste time on lies. He knows it is no use accusing you of what you haven't done. That's why his accusations hurt so much. Our response to that kind of attack must be swift and certain. 'Yes, I did do that, but I have been to the foot of the cross and I have repented – not just confessed, but repented, changed my mind and my whole attitude. Christ died for *me*. My sinful body has been made clean by his body and my soul washed through his most precious blood.'

Whatever tactic he uses, whatever approach, nowhere

will he seek more diligently to undermine you than in your prayer life, both personal and corporate – especially if you are an intercessor.

I have a friend – whom I will call Jane – a faithful intercessor if ever there was one. Some time ago she began to pray regularly with another lady whom I had never met. I will call her Anne. After a while I began to notice that whenever Jane spoke of Anne there was a certain uneasiness in her manner. Their prayer times usually took place in Jane's house and one day she confided in me that they really were becoming a bit of a problem. Anne would stay for hours, well past the time convenient for Jane, and there had been no agreement about this. Furthermore, it transpired that Jane had not been too keen on the arrangement to begin with. When I enquired why she didn't just tell Anne all this and suggest they seek the Lord together as to whether he wanted them to continue, she said, 'Oh, I've tried, but she's always so positive, so certain. She always has so much to pray about and she makes me feel I'm letting the side down. She is so much more spiritual than I am and she's always got a scriptural answer to my doubts.'

Oh dear! Jane was the victim of one of Satan's most subtle devices – to make us feel unworthy in prayer and less worthy than someone else. The answer is to look at Jesus' dealings with people and to notice that he always lifted them up. If you ever begin to feel 'put down', or start comparing yourself unfavourably with someone else, especially in spiritual matters, look out! The enemy is at work. Satan had obviously been having some success with Anne, too, but as far as Jane was concerned, once she became aware of what was really happening she was encouraged to break loose from this unsatisfactory relationship, and to realize her own worth.

There is, of course, all the difference in the world between this kind of subtle, condemnatory activity and gentle, prayerful and loving correction or advice from another Christian, especially from those set over us in the Lord.

What then is to be done about all this? How do we deal with the attacks of the enemy against us personally? Prevention is always better than cure, so preparation is our first consideration.

In chapter 4 I dealt quite fully with the spiritual armour with which God has provided us, both for protection and attack, and this may be – indeed should be – applied and used all the time in our daily lives. It is no good waiting until battle commences before we reach for it. By that time it may well be too late. We must appropriate all these things daily and constantly, and as we do so we shall be allowing the Holy Spirit to train us in their use (Ps 18:34-39). The girdle of truth, the breastplate of righteousness, the shoes of the gospel of peace and the helmet of salvation, together with the shield of faith and the sword of the Spirit, are our clothing and equipment. Turn to the word of God and meditate upon what they are and what they mean to you. Understand why it is that they are so effective.

Our very best preparation and defence against the enemy is to know God. Therefore wait upon him diligently with prayer and fasting, for used together these help tremendously in concentrating the mind upon him alone and make us open to the revelation of his will and purpose for us. The better we know God and the more we understand his ways and who he is, the less likely we are to be deceived by Satan or taken by surprise and terrified by his attacks.

A lady was talking to me recently about prayer and about listening to God and wanting to do his will. 'But,' she added, 'how do I know it is God speaking to me and not the devil, or just my own thoughts?' My answer to her was that if you love someone you want to spend time

with that person. You listen to what he says, you remember everything about him, his ideas and his attitudes, and the way he expresses himself. You get to
know him very well. If you were separated from each
other for a while you would recognize his voice on the
telephone and you would recognize the way he expressed
himself in his letters. So much so that if his voice changed
in some way, or his letters began to express things which
were not in keeping with the character of the man you
knew so well, you would be on the alert immediately.
You would know that something was wrong.

So it should be between ourselves and God, and even
more so since God longs and waits to reveal himself to us
and to make us one with himself. To this end we must be
prepared to spend much time alone with him, listening to
him and frequently meditating deeply upon the Scriptures. Take his precious word deeply into your heart, let
it sink into every fibre of your being, allowing the Holy
Spirit of God to quicken it to yourself, for instruction,
edification, guidance, encouragement and inspiration,
but most of all simply that you may *know him*.

'The word of God is living and active . . . discerning
the thoughts and intentions of the heart' (Heb 4:12). We
shall never be deceived by the wiles of the devil, or our
own thoughts, if we are steeped in that precious word,
knowing him, to whose eyes 'all are open and laid bare'
(Heb 4:13).

'Thy word is a lamp to my feet and a light to my path'
(Ps 119:105). We shall not be led astray as long as we
follow that lamp and walk in that light.

'The saying is sure and worthy of full acceptance, that
Christ Jesus came into the world to save sinners' (1 Tim
1:15).

'Christ died for our sins' (1 Cor 15:3).

'The blood of Jesus . . . cleanses us from all sin' (1 Jn
1:7).

Even the accusations of Satan that are grounded in truth turn to ashes in his mouth at these words.

And when the enemy does come upon us we shall turn, with the sword of the Spirit gleaming bright, and pierce him through with the words, 'It is written . . .' (see Lk 4:1-13).

He will attack you, you may be sure of that, but you will be ready for him, and this readiness, this closeness to God, this knowing him, is the most vital thing, not only for our own defence against the enemy, but for our effectiveness as intercessors. Whatever we may do in our groups, or in our lonely intercession, it all starts with our personal association with God. It is here, alone with God, and our eyes fixed upon him, meditating deeply upon his word, that we come to a full understanding of the truth of who he is; of what he has done for us in Christ, of the total effectiveness of the blood of Jesus and the power and authority of his blessed name. In that power and with that authority we may rebuke Satan and send him from us.

'Beloved, do not be surprised at the fiery ordeal which comes upon you to prove you, as though something strange were happening to you. But rejoice . . .' (1 Pet 4:12).

Rejoice? Yes, rejoice! And take heart. If you are attracting the attentions of Satan it is because you are effective, because you are known in hell, and we need to be known there. Remember the sons of Sceva (Acts 19:14ff), to whom the evil spirit said, 'Jesus I know, and Paul I know; but who are you?' It is not enough to have our names recorded in Heaven; we want the inhabitants of hell to have to say to us, 'We know you too, because we feel the power and the authority of Christ within you.'

I do not think we have any right to expect that we shall be spared the times of testing, nor do I think Peter would have referred to them as the 'fiery ordeal', or spoken of us having to suffer various trials 'for a little while', if they were going to be over in the twinkling of an eye. Consider the story of Daniel in the lions' den. Those lions did not disappear. Daniel told the King in the morning that God had sent his angel to shut the lions' mouths, but I do not doubt that they would have prowled up and down, giving the occasional roar, and sniffing inquisitively at Daniel from time to time throughout that long night. 'So Daniel was taken up out of the den, and no kind of hurt was found upon him, because he trusted in his God' (Dan 6:23).

Or consider Shadrach, Meshach and Abednego, tied up and cast into the furnace so hot that 'the flame of fire slew those men who took up Shadrach, Meshach and Abednego' (Dan 3:22). What happened? The fire was not quenched, but Nebuchadnezzar himself saw those three men walking freely in the midst of the fire without harm. With them was another whose appearance was 'like a son of the gods'.

'Then Nebuchadnezzar came near to the door of the burning fiery furnace and said, "Shadrach, Meshach, and Abednego, servants of the Most High God, come forth, and come here!" Then they came out from the fire. And the Satraps, the prefects, the governors, and the king's counsellors gathered together and saw that the fire had not had any power over the bodies of those men; the hair of their heads was not singed, their mantles were not harmed, and no smell of fire had come upon them. Nebuchadnezzar said, "Blessed be the God of Shadrach, Meshach and Abednego, who has sent his angel and delivered his servants, who trusted in him"' (Dan 3:26-28).

So may it be with us.

The writing of this book has not been without its hazards and I have received the personal attention of Satan several times during the course of it. Self-doubt, lack of confidence, and sometimes headaches and depression are all things I have had to deal with. A major practical setback was a very severe attack of flu. Not only was I in bed for six days myself, but the whole household went down with it too. We were a sorry sight to behold, but we ministered to each other, cheered one another up and enjoyed more of one another's company than we normally have time to do, so there were some compensations. While I was recovering I received a very welcome telephone call from a friend I hadn't heard from for a long time, and I mentioned the fact that we all had flu. 'Oh,' she said, 'so you're not living in victory then!' Well, really! I felt quite vexed with her (though I didn't say so) and just for a minute she almost had me apologizing for my influenza!

We share the common lot of all mankind and sickness is part of that common lot. Some will tell you that sickness and disease came into the world through sin, but however it came, here it is. I am not denying the power of God to heal, but Jesus did not pray that his disciples (and that means us too) should be spared the normal experience of living in this world as it is. 'I do not pray that thou shouldst take them out of the world, but that thou shouldst keep them from the evil one' (Jn 17:15).

The important thing is not that we should be miraculously spared the ordinary experiences of human life, including sickness, bereavement, and hardships of various kinds, or even the unwelcome attentions of the devil, but that we should pass through them in safety.

> When you pass through the waters I will be with you; and
> through the rivers, they shall not overwhelm you;
> when you walk through fire you shall not be burned, and the
> flame shall not consume you (Is 43:2).

We shall come forth, and no kind of hurt shall be found upon us – no, not even the smell of burning.

So let us praise the Most High God who delivers his servants who trust in him! And let Satan and all the inhabitants of hell clearly hear us testify that Jesus Christ is Lord! Our praises and the word of our testimony are more than they can stand.

Praise God in every situation. However dire the circumstances, God is still God. Jesus is Lord! However Satan may attack us, his ultimate purpose is simply to separate us from God. Our praises not only glorify God, they keep us mindful of who he is and signify to the enemy that he has failed. I know full well that it isn't easy to begin to praise God when the going is rough, but it gets easier once we've started, and it is easier with a little help from our friends. It is always a good idea, when under attack, to call up reinforcements if we can, that is, to ask one or two friends to pray for us. So next time this happens to you, try asking them to join you in a few paeans of praise! It will be wonderfully effective!

As you do so you will experience another of the Holy Spirit's surprises – *joy!* The great joy that will well up inside you because you will know the power of the living God within you, the sweetness of the presence of Jesus as he walks with you through the fiery ordeal.

> Bless the Lord, O my soul; and all that is within me bless his holy name   (Ps 103:1).

> Praise the Lord, O my soul!
> I will praise the Lord as long as I live;
> I will sing praises to my God while I have being (Ps 146:1-2).

> Thou, O Lord, art a shield about me, my glory, and the lifter of my head   (Ps 3:3).

PART THREE

A Many Splendoured Thing

12

New Ways of Praying

To set out on the way of an intercessor is to embark upon an adventure.

In the first chapter I described this 'way' as 'sacrificial, disciplined, at times dangerous . . .', all of which it is, but this is not the whole story. Like any adventure, this one is full of surprises – the Holy Spirit's surprises in this case. If we will trust him and allow him to lead us, he will teach us many unexpected and exciting things in the way of prayer.

Perhaps you have recognized the title of this section. A songwriter used these words to describe love, but I am applying them to this incredibly varied activity which we call prayer. There are so many facets to prayer that the illustration of a precious gemstone is very appropriate. Each facet of prayer reflects the Light differently, giving glory back to the One who motivates, inspires and directs our prayer. Truly, a many splendoured thing.

To many of us, the new things we have learnt in prayer as a result of the outpouring of the Holy Spirit have come as a real surprise, and some people have been fearful and reluctant to learn. We need have no fear. God is the same yesterday, today and for ever, and these seemingly new things are really the everlasting ways of the Spirit in prayer. They are new to some of us simply be-

NEW WAYS OF PRAYING

cause they have been overlaid by other things, other traditions, in the ways of the church, and not experienced by us until now.

Live, Spirit-directed prayer really is the fourth dimension to life. We can't touch it, weigh it, measure it, or analyse how God uses it. It is a mystery, which the dictionary defines as an aspect, especially of Christianity, beyond human understanding. As God's power to work through our prayer cannot be bound by the limits of our human understanding, so we ought not to limit the expression of that prayer by a fearful unwillingness to be led by him.

It is not surprising that people who have always prayed in a certain way, perhaps with their eyes shut and their hands together, should be wary of any suggestion that they might do something different, like raising their arms, for example. To begin with they probably can't see any reason why they should, and anyone who has never done it cannot be expected to appreciate the benefits of expressing prayer in different ways. It is only as we make the first hesitant experiments that we begin to experience the glorious freedom which the Holy Spirit gives us. On the last day of a residential conference a few years ago, a lady testified to how much it had meant to her to experience movement in prayer and worship in one of the Movement Workshops we had had, but she began by saying that when she arrived at the conference she was certain she would never take part in the 'dreaded dance' as she called it! Little did she know, on that first day, that before the end of the conference the 'dreaded dance' would release her into new joy and freedom!

When I first heard of people dancing in church my reaction was very cautious. Certainly I knew that David danced before the Lord (2 Sam 6:14), but that was in biblical times, and Old Testament times at that!

The Bible does, in fact, contain a number of references to prayer which indicate that kneeling was not the only suitable posture for prayer. A whole congregation fell on their faces before the Lord (Num 16:22), as did Joshua (Josh 5:14), David and the elders (1 Chron 21:16) and Jesus himself (Mt 26:39).

Bowing down is mentioned (Ps 95:6), lifting up the hands (Ps 28:2; Lam 2:19; 1 Tim 2:8), and spreading forth the hands (Is 1:15), and the psalmist testifies that even his mourning has been turned into *dancing* (Ps 30:11).

Because we are all unique personalities, the Holy Spirit may lead us in different ways. His variety is infinite and what is appropriate for one may not be so for another. He is always very gentle with us, never compelling us to do anything, but rather inviting us to surrender our whole being – body, as well as mind and spirit – to him, and to enter into freedom in worship and prayer.

What is appropriate in one prayer situation will not necessarily be so in another, though there is no telling where the Holy Spirit will lead. This applies to times of corporate prayer as much as to individual times. As always, what is necessary is sensitivity to his direction and a willingness to learn.

What I share now are some of the things I have learnt, and am still learning, in company with other Christians and fellow intercessors. Although I am only able to say a little about each facet, I hope it will be enough to get you moving, to inspire and encourage you to experiment under the guidance of the Holy Spirit – to respond, not only to movement, but to the other deep things of prayer which he will bring to you.

'Lord, teach us to pray.'

13

The Prayer of the Body – Movement and Stillness

I put this first for the reason that it is often movement, albeit just a slight gesture, with which we first indicate our willingness to respond, either to God or to each other.

Reconciliation often begins with reaching out a hand, or just turning to look at someone. When we are being resistant to change, to God, or to each other, we stiffen up, maintaining our present position. We are sitting still metaphorically if not actually, and we have to move in some way in order to change things. It is quite amazing how much can come from a small movement. An outstretched hand may give rise to a flood of repentance, forgiveness and reconciliation, or in comfort, reassurance and encouragement.

One of the biggest mistakes we make, in my opinion, is in trying to departmentalize ourselves. Body, mind and spirit we think of separately, and though most of us are fairly happy with a merger between mind and spirit, somehow the body becomes the poor relation. The ills which afflict the body, and the evil uses to which it may be put, are continually before our eyes, so perhaps our reluctance to use our bodies in worship and prayer springs partly from a feeling that they are not worthy. Or perhaps we are too conscious of their temporal nature.

While we live on earth, however, we have a physical body. We are a complete human being – body, mind and spirit together. Paul exhorted the Corinthians to 'glorify God in your body' (1 Cor 6:20), and to the Romans he wrote, 'I appeal to you therefore, brethren, by the mercies of God, to present your bodies as a living sacrifice, holy and acceptable to God, which is your spiritual worship' (Rom 12:1). He also advised the Corinthians that the body is meant for the Lord, and asked them, 'Do you not know that your bodies are members of Christ?' and 'a temple of the Holy Spirit' (1 Cor 6:15, 19).

Therefore we should honour our bodies, look after them and use them to God's glory. Keeping them fit and learning to relax, and therefore not being too tired or tense to pray, are elementary necessities. Failure to attend to these things may well result not only in discomfort for our bodies, but dullness of our minds and the imprisonment of our spirits. At the very least we need to make sure that our bodies do not interfere with our prayer. So if you have never done this before, may I suggest that you now begin to practice relaxing? Take some deep breaths, loosen your limbs, and remember the introduction to a certain radio programme for children: 'Are you sitting comfortably?'

Begin, if you can, to be aware of your body as an instrument, a means of expressing yourself as effectively as you can with your voice, for the body does indeed provide us with another language. Just as the Holy Spirit will give us another verbal language – speaking in tongues – so he will also give us a very beautiful and effective body language.

You will notice that I have used the word 'movement', and not 'dance', in the heading of this chapter. This is because dance is only a part of the whole experience – albeit a very important part – of movement in worship and prayer. You may have seen some of the wonderful dance presentations of groups like the Sacred Dance Group from Dorset, and for many of us this kind of presentation is our first introduction to movement in worship. What an exciting and enriching ministry this is. However, what I am mostly concerned with here is our personal activity – we are not all 'dancers' in the usual interpretation of that word – and with how movement may be used in our groups.

Although you may not consider yourself to be a dancer, it may help to begin by moving to music. You probably have a record or cassette of some praise and worship songs. Select one that suits your need at the moment and as you listen to it allow the Holy Spirit to interpret it for you in terms of movement. You may be surprised and delighted at what follows! One point I would like to stress, however. Don't do it as a kind of intellectual exercise. That will get you nowhere. At the first Movement Work- shop I attended we were told by the leader that there would be no spectators. All were encouraged to join in, for although we were learners this was to be an act of worship and prayer from the start. I was fascinated by the prospect of this new dimension, but rather diffident. I felt like the Rock of Gibralter, solid and immovable, but not for long. I soon forgot about everyone else and my own imaginary limitations, as I allowed the Holy Spirit, assisted in this case by our leader, to inspire me and *move* me! So let even your first experiment be a real offering to God. Most of us respond to music (even a tiny toddler will bounce up and down or sway to its rhythm), so this is a very helpful way to start.

Recently I attended a day seminar at Longmead, the home of the Sacred Dance Group, where I was surprised and delighted to discover there were those among us who had been praising, worshipping and praying with dance in the privacy of their own rooms. 'Secret dancers' indeed. For many of them this had been the result of their own spontaneous response to the prompting of the Holy Spirit. How blessed are they who are able to respond with childlike, unselfconscious simplicity to his invitation! Incidentally, they were not all women either!

The discovery of the body as an instrument of worship can be a delightful bonus to one particular group of people – the non-singers among us. As one who has been a singer in choirs since I was very young I didn't appreciate this until a friend of mine who is tone deaf and croaks like a frog (her description, not mine!) told me what a joy it is for her to be able to express and interpret all the lovely songs with her body. Isn't God gracious?

When I began to learn how to pray with my body I found it helpful to look, for example, at my hands, to observe how I could manipulate them and to consider how they could be used. I learnt that they could be held out to God in a gesture of receiving, or of offering; they may be cupped in adoration, as though I held and gazed into the face of Jesus; they could be held, arms outstretched in front of me, palms outwards, as an expression of rejection (of my sin, for example), or lifted high, palms raised, in an act of worship and acclamation. Or my arms could be folded across my chest, head bowed, in a position of penitence, or grief. All these positions may be adopted either standing or kneeling.

Gradually I learnt to move and to take up other positions as the Holy Spirit prompted me; to kneel and bow my head to the ground in reverence, or again in sorrow for my sin; to prostrate myself with arms outstretched, in awe and amazement before the majesty of God, or in supplication; to stretch out my arms sideways in an act of intercession. It was at a Lydia conference that I was first introduced to the idea of the body as a vehicle for intercession, and this extended the boundaries of my experience still further, for I learnt that as well as adopting the by then familiar movements and positions already described, I could use my body to express whatever emotion, desire or entreaty the Holy Spirit might give me as he directed my prayer. This part of the prayer of movement I believe to be very personal.

Some of the positions and movements I have mentioned, and others, may be described as classic since they have been used by Christians for centuries, but this further expression of the prayer inspired by the Holy Spirit at a particular time and for a particular purpose, has much in common with prayer in a 'tongue', in that it is for our own personal use, and it enables us to give expression to the deepest cries of our hearts when ordinary language fails. For this reason it is the Holy Spirit himself who must be our teacher. Others can encourage us and inspire us to be free and open to his direction, but ultimately he is the One who will give us our own personal body language.

As in all things, the Holy Spirit never compels us, he just invites us, but our ready response and willingness to learn take us deeper into the heart of God, into closer co-operation with him in the way of prayer.

How far this kind of prayer may be used in your intercession groups will depend upon you. The use of dance and movement, or even different postures, in larger gatherings or in church, are a matter for the ministers, pastors and people concerned to consider, as God moves them to do so, but in a small group of intercessors this may easily become a valuable and normal part of the expression of your prayer. Sensitivity to one another, as well as to the promptings of the Holy Spirit, is essential as you begin to venture into this new way of praying.

The way of prayer for the body includes stillness as well as movement, and I have often found that a period of complete stillness follows the physical expression of my prayer. This may be a time for holding and consolidating what God has just given in movement, or it may be just for relaxing and being with God. This is a very precious time, and it is good to sit in a comfortable chair which supports you, or to lie upon the floor, so that every muscle of your body may be relaxed. In this position you may consciously let go of all the tensions and worries, all the cares and duties of your life, and just be aware of God who is within you (Jn 14:23), rejoicing in the sweetness of his presence and allowing him to fill you with his healing, strengthening and encouraging grace. Your body may also in this way speak to him of your complete surrender to his will for you, your willingness to be used by him in prayer.

I remember vividly how I struggled for a long time with a hard decision I knew God was requiring me to make, until one day, when I was lying face down upon the ground before him, I just turned over and lay there on my back with my arms outstretched. I didn't speak a word, but in that stillness, that position of surrender, my body said it all.

Perhaps you are wondering now what about people who are sick, or handicapped, who cannot get up and move? Just as God can take even the damaged body and mould it into that 'complete system' which is the holy person, so too he will enable the sick or the handicapped body to give glory to him. One of the loveliest things I have ever seen was a severely crippled young woman at a Movement Workshop. She could not stand without assistance, but she did what she could from her chair. For the rest, her total acceptance of her situation, her complete lack of self-pity and her enjoyment of the praise and worship, shone through the repose of her body and the expression on her face.

Perhaps most of all in the lovely stillness we may be acknowledging and expressing the most important thing of all, that it is God alone who matters – not our working, our loving, even our precious ministry of intercession, but himself. If he asks me to stay right here and be a 'nothing', then that is what I'll be. In this place of deep, self-forgetful intimacy with him we come face to face with a wonder, another mystery, that the mighty, powerful, Most High God who created all things and holds all things in being, is the same God who loves us with the most tender, compassionate love, and has a concern for every detail of our lives. We may begin to understand that the fruitfulness of all we do for him; all our reading and meditating upon his word; our learning; our listening; our praying; our growing towards maturity and holiness; all this depends ultimately upon our closeness to our Lord, upon this giving of ourselves to him and himself to us, so that the light of his presence shines through even our mortal bodies.

'Abide in me, and I in you' (Jn 15:4).

14

Tongues

He that speaketh in an unknown tongue speaketh not unto men, but unto God' (1 Cor 14:2 AV).

There are several specific references in the New Testament to the gift of tongues, beginning with our Lord's own words, 'These signs will accompany those who believe . . . they will speak in new tongues' (Mk 16:17), and it is apparent that this was one of the commonest manifestations of the outpouring of the Holy Spirit upon the early church.

There is evidence also that this gift was expected and used at least until the fourth century, at which time St Augustine of Hippo wrote that new converts were expected to speak with new tongues at the laying on of hands. The fact that this gift has been largely ignored, or even positively rejected by the church since those times, has given rise to some confusion now that a fresh outpouring of the Holy Spirit has released it to be used by many people once more. However, a study of how it occurred in the early church, as related in Acts; or Paul's references to it in his Epistle to the Corinthians and especially his admonitions concerning its use; and of the current experience of many mature and responsible Christians, reveals that it is given and used in the following ways:

As a sign – to those who do not believe.

As an indication of the presence of the Holy Spirit, especially following the initial receiving of the Spirit (Acts 2:4; 10:44-46; 19:6).

To edify and encourage the church – when followed by interpretation (1 Cor 12:10; 14:13).

To magnify God (Acts 10:46).

For worship.

For prayer and praise.

Anyone not already familiar with this gift will find several helpful books or booklets available. *Speaking in Tongues – A Gift for the Church* by Larry Christensen, originally published by Fountain Trust, is one. The subject is also dealt with in a very helpful booklet called *The Gifts of the Spirit* by Roy Parsons, published by Anglicans for Renewal and available from 441 Upper Elmers End Road, Beckenham BR3 3DB.

One of the most fascinating books about this gift is *They Speak with Other Tongues* by John Sherrill (Hodder & Stoughton; now Highland Books), in which he tells how, as a journalist and a conventional Episcopalian, he set out to make an objective study of this phenomenon, and how his researches led to his being filled with the Holy Spirit and speaking in tongues himself!

Once again God does not impose his gift upon us, but it is available to us, and in my experience he is so gracious in the way he leads us into new experiences. When I had been filled with the Spirit and had discovered that there was such a thing as the gift of tongues I so much wanted to have it and use it, but somehow I didn't seem able to appropriate it. After reading a really quite funny account of how one man sat at his desk and waited in vain for the sounds to come, I realized, as he had done, that it was up to me to start using this gift. Since I had asked him for it, God had already given it to me, but still I couldn't do it. Eventually, at a prayer meeting one evening, God helped me gently over the hurdle. During a time of praise and worship people all around me were quietly singing in the Spirit and my heart was full of love, praise and joy. How long I had been singing in a new tongue before I stopped to think about what I was doing I do not know, but there I was happily praising God – singing unto the Lord a new song! Of course the Lord knew very well that to sing was as natural to me as breathing, so he chose that way to overcome my difficulties!

Since that happy day I have learnt to use this beautiful and useful gift in my private times of prayer. It enables me to praise God and worship him when the ordinary words of my mother tongue are inadequate – which is often! I can pray when the exact circumstances of a situation are unknown to me, or when the deep stirrings of the Spirit within me can be expressed in no other way. I often use it when I am suddenly confronted by an unexpected situation, or in an emergency when there is no time to think. I just give the situation to God and pray in the Spirit. I also use it as a weapon against Satan, and very powerful it is too.

Paul said that when he prayed in the Spirit his mind was unfruitful, and from my own experience I understand that my mind contributes nothing to this kind of prayer, which means that for as long as I do pray in this way it may be concentrated upon God alone, while the Spirit himself makes the prayer.

Only once during the good number of years since I first received it, has God required me to use a tongue publicly, when of course it had to be followed by an interpretation.

We may expect to experience and use the gift of tongues in all these ways in our time of intercession together. As we worship we may allow the Holy Spirit to lead us beyond what is possible with our ordinary language in the expression of our love and adoration, and as we glorify God in this way we ourselves are inspired and encouraged to praise him more. Sometimes he will give us the music to go with our tongues, so that we magnify him in song also.

During our preparation, for example when assisting one another to lay down our burdens, we may sometimes pray the 'holding' prayer in tongues, especially if someone has a burden which it is difficult to share specifically. The Holy Spirit knows, and he will pray through us.

We may use it when addressing Satan, in our preparation or during our time of intercession, binding him, and declaring the lordship of Jesus. Remember that the weapons we are to use in our fight against Satan are not worldly ones (2 Cor 10:4). This gift of tongues is a mighty and powerful weapon in spiritual warfare, since it is the Holy Spirit himself who is active in its use.

Normally a tongue is only meant to be heard by others when God also gives an interpretation for the edification and encouragement of all, but I think that in a small group of this kind it is acceptable to pray audibly, but quietly, in the Spirit. Once again the key word is sensitivity to God and to one another.

Finally, God may give direction in prayer through a tongue followed by an interpretation, and in this way he may also give encouragement and confirmation of what is being achieved in the spiritual realms.

Accept this gift as a normal part of your prayer life, alone and together, and use it with confidence in conjunction with all the other ways of praying, remembering that it is given not simply for our own self-gratification, but for the good of others and to the glory of God.

> I will pray with the spirit and I will pray with the mind also; I will sing with the spirit and I will sing with the mind also (1 Cor 14:15).

15

The Prayer of Identification

> Rejoice with those who rejoice, weep with those who weep (Rom 12:15).

To become a true intercessor is to make yourself vulnerable. It means that regardless of your own circumstances you are ready and willing to experience, as fully as God gives you grace to do so, the pain and the suffering (as well as the joys), of other people. It means too that you are prepared to let God decide who those other people shall be.

If you are going to pray sincerely: 'Lord, give me grace inside to love the world like you. Lord, give me grace to give my life away,' you are going to say to him that there is nothing and no one from whom you will shrink back. You are going to be totally available to him and to the world. You are going to learn the full meaning of the words 'sympathy' and 'compassion', to feel and to share the grief, sorrow and misery of other people, to be spiritually identified with them, and by your identification to offer the prayer of intercession for them.

How can this be? How can our willingness to feel their pain be of any use to them or to God? Once again we are face to face with mystery, something beyond our human understanding, but nevertheless something which we have to accept as we follow the way of an intercessor. If we cannot come to terms with this we shall not travel very far along the way. This mysterious experience of identification is right at the heart of the ministry of intercession, even when what is happening to those for whom we pray is outside our own experience. I don't know how God uses this prayer, and I don't suppose anyone else does either, but that doesn't matter. What does matter is that, in this as in everything else, we should be willing to receive what he is currently teaching us and that we should be found faithful in our response.

Food has always been something of a problem for me. Not only because I like it, but because in the past it has been for me a comfort. I believe psychiatrists call it 'compensation eating'. A baby sucks his thumb, one person lights up a cigarette, and another eats for comfort! However, we must all learn to find our consolation in the Lord.

Some time ago I was holding this problem of mine before him, and on several occasions during my times of prayer I found myself thinking that there are a lot of people starving in the world. These thoughts persisted until I realized that God was telling me something. I felt that he was asking me to go without the sweet, comforting foods I enjoyed so much. As I did so I would be identifying in a small way with the poor and the starving, and making a prayer for them. This would be a love offering for them. Further, he directed my thoughts to Colossians 2:6-7, which in the Living Bible reads as follows: 'Trust him, too, for each day's problems; live in vital union with him. Let your roots grow down into him and *draw up nourishment from him.* See that you go on growing in the Lord, and *become strong and vigorous* in the truth.' (Italics mine.) What he was telling me was that there would be no loss in this for me. On the contrary, I was to trust *him,* find my consolation in *him,* and from him I would receive all the nourishment, strength and vigour I needed.

I should like to be able to tell you that I did just as he said, that I immediately stopped indulging in sweet and tasty foods, and that I went on to grow in understanding and strength in my prayer of identification. Alas, it was not so! For a few days – about three, I think – I endeavoured to do what I believed the Lord was setting before me, but this was such a new idea and I had never heard anyone speak of making a prayer in this way, so it wasn't long before doubt crept in and I began to feel a little foolish. My endeavour tailed off, and eventually ceased altogether.

About a week later reports began to appear in the news concerning the women and children who were starving to death in a certain African country which was currently suffering war and revolution. On to our television screen one night flashed pictures of these suffering people, and they hit me almost like a physical blow! God said to me in that moment, *'These* are the people I wanted you to pray for.'

You can say, if you like, that this was just an emotional and quite natural response to the sight of such suffering, but I knew then, and I know now, that God had wanted me to identify with those people. This would have been my first conscious experience of the prayer of identification, had I followed him down the path which he indicated. My failure taught me a lesson I cannot forget.

A woman I know described how she had tried in vain to pray for a certain person who for a long time had been depressed and feeling 'persecuted'. Shortly afterwards she had one of those days when everything went wrong that could go wrong; everything and everybody seemed to be against her and she felt cross and resentful. Then she realized that the person for whom she wanted to pray must be feeling like this nearly all the time. She was being permitted to share, just for a little while, the suffering of that other person. This was her prayer.

I believe God asks us to pray in this way more often than we realize. Often, even in our ordinary everyday life, we are made aware of the suffering of other people. We meet people who have a problem of some kind and we allow their experience to impinge upon our life just so much and no more, but if as intercessors we are sensitive to the promptings of the Holy Spirit we shall find ourselves opening our hearts and allowing their pain to enter as fully as is possible into our own experience. We are to be vulnerable. We must understand, too, that the people for whom God asks us to pray in this way may not necessarily be those we like and those with whom we have a natural sympathy. Our brother is 'any man'. Our sister is 'any woman'. We are to be unconditionally available.

> Enlarge the place of your tent, and let the curtains of your habitations be stretched out; hold not back, lengthen your cords and strengthen your stakes (Is 54:2).

This prayer of identification may find its expression in many ways, but there are two things which often accompany it, or indeed are its expression.

The first is weeping. Don't ever be ashamed or afraid of tears, they are a precious gift of the Holy Spirit, and a means whereby we can sometimes give expression to things too deeply felt for words or actions. At a certain time in my life I was made aware of how my sin had grievously hurt someone else and I was deeply sorry, but the pain in my heart was not only sorrow for my sin, it was grief for the other person's pain which I was briefly permitted to share. I would have prayed for that person if I could, but I had no prayer. Then came the tears. I remember sitting perfectly still, not sobbing or making any sound, with this dreadful ache in my heart and the tears pouring silently from me. That was my prayer. It was the only one I had to offer and it was acceptable to God. I believe he used it.

The second is the silent heartcry. When there are no words, no gestures and no tears, the response of our heart is, in some mysterious way, our prayer. It may be that we can take the person or the people God is laying on our hearts and simply hold them before him, allowing their pain, their sorrow, to cry to him through us, and this becomes our prayer. And this silent cry of the heart is a prayer we can offer to him continually, throughout the day, whatever we are doing. When we are not able to go to our place of prayer nor offer to him the more tangible prayers, this may continue.

> Let tears stream down like a torrent . . . Pour out your heart like water before the presence of the Lord (Lam 2:18-19).

'Rejoice with those who rejoice,' said Paul, as well as 'weep with those who weep', and this is the other side of the prayer of identification. To 'feel with' someone, to be associated with them, may equally well be to share and to experience their happiness. If our hearts are open to pain and grief they are also open to joy and gladness. Just as we may weep with someone, so also may we laugh. We may offer up to God true thankfulness and praise from a heart that is truly 'feeling with' another. Even tears, so often the expression of the grief we feel with another, may at other times be the expression of deep joy, or the outward and visible sign, expressed by us, of spiritual release or renewal experienced by them.

It is not easy to write about the deep, mysterious things of prayer, for they are given by the Spirit to each of us as he wills and must be spiritually received and understood. What is necessary is that we open our hearts to the Spirit of God, without fear or reservation. Then we shall be caught up in the wonder of oneness with him, as we begin to share and express his love and compassion for the whole world.

Lord, teach us to pray.